EACH PERSON
MUST LIVE
THEIR LIFE AS A
MODEL
FOR OTHERS.

LEADERS OF INDIA

業務部

THIS BOOK BELONGS TO

_____

_____

DECORATE *workshop*

A creative 8 step process for transforming your home

Holly Becker founder of decor8blog.com

with photography by Debi Treloar

jacqui
small

This book is dedicated to my readers and students, whom
I love dearly. Thank you for supporting me in all that I do.
Your friendship and love is the wind in my sail.

First published in 2012 by
Jacqui Small LLP an imprint of
Aurum Press Ltd
7 Greenland Street
London NW1 0ND

Text copyright © Holly Becker 2012
Photography, design and layout
copyright © Jacqui Small LLP 2012

ISBN 978 1 906417 77 2

A catalogue record for this book is
available from the British Library.

2014 2013 2012
10 9 8 7 6 5 4 3 2 1

Printed in China

PUBLISHER Jacqui Small
MANAGING EDITOR Kerenza Swift
PROJECT EDITOR Sian Parkhouse
DESIGNER Sarah Rock
STYLIST Holly Becker
ILLUSTRATOR Samantha Hahn
PRODUCTION Peter Colley

contents

Decorate with me

It is my sincere invitation that you'll join me in this interactive workshop to explore creativity, self-expression, personalization and a 'try anything once' approach to decorating. Your home should be an authentic expression of who you are, who you hope to become and it should honour your roots because they have made you exactly who you are today – and that's something worth cherishing and sharing with others.

Let's face it, everything is better in life with a good friend by your side. When I decide to work on a project I find it beneficial to tap into a knowledgeable friend who is willing to share pointers and even cheer me on along the way. This book is my hand reaching out for yours as I lead you

' When you tap into your creative side, everything is enhanced and decorating is really just that – being creative in your home in a very personal way. '

down a happy path, free of judgement, bossiness and pretension, as we work on your next decorating project in eight steps together. You're not alone. I've provided several writing prompts to inspire and motivate you along the way because I want to encourage you to finish what you've started. Your vision deserves to see the light of day so that you can walk into your home and say that it feels 'just right'. I'm here to help make that happen.

Everyone wants to feel at home yet often it is the first thing that we neglect when busy schedules overcrowd our lives. Decorating is an act of creative self-expression, which is why it's most often pushed to the side simply because creativity is not revered in

most societies or seen as a necessity – being practical and rational is. Exercising our creative side is viewed as a luxury, a bonus, something that we can tap into only when we've finished everything else. I don't buy into that for one second. I encourage you to schedule time each week for creative expression in the home – because we all have a creative side, we simply need to engage it.

This book goes a bit further than 'Put that sofa there and place these lamps on either side.' I will guide you first on a mini self-discovery mission, then I'll share how to view everyday things with a more creative eye. Next you'll be shown how to build out some of your ideas in a more tangible way and from there I'll provide lots of decorating guidelines and examples, and finally you will be on your way to doing all sorts of lovely things to your home. That's how I approach decorating from start to finish – to tap in and then connect the mind with the home.

When I decided to write a second book to follow *Decorate*, I felt strongly that I needed to give you a book that I myself had long wished to find but couldn't – a decorating guide that I could write in and put to good use. It's often scary to write in books, I get that. Mainly because books feel quite precious and so much heart, soul, time and money goes into the making of them. The thing is, I was a blogger long before I became an author and I can't imagine writing a blog that no one ever commented on. My approach for this book is very much like blogging, that we're involved in a conversation – I'm voicing my opinion and you're responding. I invite

' The making of a home is an ongoing process, it's like a never-ending art project and, most importantly; it should be fun. '

' My approach for this book is very much like blogging, that we're involved in a conversation – I'm voicing my opinion and you're responding. '

you to relax, grab a pencil with a good eraser (in case you need to modify something along the way) and give yourself the freedom and permission to use this interactive guide to your best advantage. Write in it! Highlight parts that speak to you with a fat yellow marker, make notes in the columns with a pencil or ball-point pen, sketch, doodle, respond to the various prompts that I've left that will allow you to explore your inner decorator. Instead of viewing this as writing *in* a book, view this as writing *a* book in which I am the author and you are my co-author.

I believe that the ultimate compliment is when someone steps into your home and says, 'This is so you, I love what you've done here!' Making something your own is really the spice of life – the seasoning on the beautifully prepared meal, a meal that you want to share with others because you are proud of your creation. A home should be the same, and this can be accomplished by allowing yourself to communicate your vision – an inspiring act in itself. I believe being house proud fuels all areas of our lives, trickling into the biggies like our self-esteem, comfort, security, family relationships and how safe we feel in our own skin. My belief is that when your foundation, namely your home, feels right then everything else just works better. Even when hard times come at least the security and warmth we feel at home coupled with our comfy bed and a big squishy pillow to cry into, makes difficult moments more bearable.

When you tap into your creative side, everything is enhanced and decorating is really just that – being creative in your home in a very personal way. The making of a home is an ongoing process, it's like a never-ending art project and most importantly, it should be fun. Through the pages of this book you'll be encouraged to explore your decorating

approach through fresh eyes while enjoying the process because the journey should be as sweet as the destination. We're a team and I wholeheartedly believe that together we can make your home a little sweeter. Want to get started? Good, I was hoping you'd say that.

Holly Becker

What do you need to get started?

Before we begin working on my eight steps, I thought we should first put some key things in place. The first is a creative exercise that involves only a few magazines and an hour of your time. Pull together a few style files to get your decorating gears turning. Style files are simply manilla file folders that are labelled by room name such as 'Bedroom' or 'Dining Room'. Pull some pages of rooms from magazines and catalogues that speak to you and place them in your folders. This exercise is meant to be fun and to light your creative spark, though later you will be referring to them again as you begin to home in on your ideas, create moodboards and develop your final room scheme. Next I would like to ask you to create a Project Binder, as outlined in the box right. Finally, please look over my Toolbox page and try to pull together as many of these items as you can. You have a great foundation on which to begin. You're already on your way!

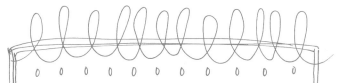

PROJECT BINDER

Keep everything in one place with a project binder. I use binders with pockets and label each section. This isn't a catch-all file for everything that crosses my desk, only what I think I will use. Label your sections in a way that works for you. I usually label mine as follows:

• • •

Floor plans –For floor plans and measurements.

• • •

Details/Swatches – This is where I insert spec sheets on specific pieces, which could be a printout of a few different sofas I'm considering along with swatches, dimensions, materials, etc. You can print out the details on specific products from the manufacturer's website, too, and insert those in this section.

• • •

Quotes – For contractor quotes, prices for furniture you're still deciding on, etc.

• • •

Contacts – This is where details of those I'm working with, from showroom sales reps to delivery services and beyond, are kept. I usually toss in their business cards or write down their contact info on a sheet of paper and place it here.

• • •

Photos – Insert photos that you've taken of your room or pieces that you know you want to use.

• • •

Invoices – For items already purchased and work that you've completed.

• • •

Lists & Spreadsheets - For instance, lists of what I want to buy for my decorating project. My General Project Overview spreadsheet, which outlines everything that I'm working on so that I can stay on plan, would also be in this part of my binder. Other spreadsheets I'd include would be one that outlines all details concerning each item that I've purchased or plan to purchase – item name, code number, supplier, contact, specs, price, availability – another for my budget, where I break down everything detailing estimates and final costs, and a spreadsheet meant for tracking all purchases that I've made to date.

• • •

Moodboards – If you have a digital moodboard, print it out in colour and place it here. If you've created one by hand, photograph it, crop the photo, reduce to letter size and print it out in colour. It's great to have a snapshot to refer to.

YOUR DECORATING TOOLBOX

- **Computer with internet access** You can access design blogs and other online resources that are both educational and inspiring, and use it to upload photos, create digital moodboards, create folders on your desktop to organize your decorating ideas, put together spreadsheets to track materials and budget, draft floor plans and source items from wallpaper to sofas and beyond.

- **Digital camera** A must for snapping photos of things that inspire you while you're out and about, but also helpful as you begin to plan your room.

- **Retractable tape measure** These are the sturdy ones builders clip to their belts. My favourites are those with an auto-locking mechanism for times when I need to measure my space alone.

- **Sewing tape measure** This is a non-stretchable flexible strip, usually in plastic or fabric, and is helpful for measuring the distance around an item.

- **Printer with a built-in scanner** If you don't fancy running to the copy shop and you don't want to own multiple machines, purchase a printer/scanner combo so that you can scan magazine tears, fabrics that you may not want to cut into to create a swatch and any other materials that you think you could use on your moodboard or you would like to access on your computer.

- **Scissors** I have several different types of scissors for both paper and fabric and a pair of pinking shears with those lovely teeth meant to prevent fraying – I really like how swatches look when cut with my pinking shears! Hey, it's the little things, right?

- **Project box or tray** This is a great place to start collecting things that you think may work for your project that are bulky. Gather tile samples, flooring, catalogues and anything else that you can think

of. You will pull from this pile later and begin the editing process but it's a great place to start accumulating your inspirations.

- **Painter's tape** Perfect to use if you need to outline where you plan to place furniture, mirrors, art, etc. You also may use it for actual painting if you decide on a new wall colour, too!

- **Pencils/erasers** I leave my pens aside when sketching floor plans because I cannot draw a straight line very well and a pencil is much more forgiving than a pen – just erase and try again!

- **Colour pencils (or watercolours)** If you want to explore colour try applying it to your floor plans. I was trained to do this on the job and later in design school and you will find it helpful if you have the time and patience.

- **Blu-tack** A staple in every stylist's bag, this putty-like adhesive is reusable and perfect for easily applying lightweight objects to dry surfaces like walls. With Blu-tack you can quickly tack up a sheet of wallpaper, painted poster boards to test colours in a room or art prints to see how they look on the wall before you have them framed.

- **Grid paper or 3D software for floor plans** You will want to keep paper around for sketching loose plans as well as for drawing to-scale plans as you go. If you have access to software that can make the job easier, by all means use it!

- **Swatches** If you are as addicted to decorating as I am you no doubt have a collection of swatches that you refer to for inspiration and as potential jumping-off points for projects. I keep them in clear folders organized by colour.

1 Seek INSPIRATION

Digging for treasure is the perfect starting point as you begin to decorate. Knowing what's out there is key as you build up an idea of what you're responding to. This step examines where to find inspiration and the value of keeping an open mind and heart as you get started. So, what inspires YOU? Let's find out!

Find your PERSONAL STYLE 2

Gathering inspiration can be never-ending – at some point you have to pull back and start to make sense of it all. It's time to focus and sift through your finds to identify key themes so you can tap into your vision. This isn't about putting a label on your style, it's simply a step meant to call out themes and decide what is 'you' and what isn't.

3 IDENTIFY your project

Once you feel motivated, inspired and on track with your personal style, you'll naturally need to look at your home and decide which room is screaming the loudest for a new look. Your budget, lifestyle and how you plan to use the room all come into play next. Where do you want to get started?

4 PREP your space

While it may sound less exciting than collecting inspiration, preparing your space is also about digging for treasure and shining up the gems that you have! As you get started on your decorating project, it's time to pull your stuff together by listing, sorting, measuring, photographing, tidying and organizing it!

DRAW UP your space

Wow, you've come a long way! With your ideas in motion and your space ready to go you can now consider your options, assess your space and draft some floor plans!

Translate your IDEAS

It's time to see how your ideas work together on paper by consolidating them through moodboards and other creative exercises. You are one step closer to nailing down your design scheme and pulling it together. Who said decorating is stressful? Not you!

FINALIZE your scheme

It's time to go from planning to execution. Next you'll pin down the details and create a scheme that works. In this step, I'll take you through some of my favourite decorating ideas for living, eating, sleeping and workspaces to see what tips you can use in your final plan. Way to go, you're almost there!

Happy DECORATING

This is when your hard work really pays off. The sofa is in place, your new bookcase has arrived . . . it's time to personalize and decorate! Consider the details, play with some pattern, edit your stuff, decide what you will display and how to style it and then step back and snap your 'after' photos – it's time to celebrate!

STEP 1

SEEK INSPIRATION

' A jumping-off point is usually a single source of inspiration that you build from because it inspires all other elements that you will pull into the room. It may be a scarf, a piece of vintage fabric, a tear sheet from a magazine or an outfit that you spotted in a catalogue. '

Welcome to the first step in your decorating journey, where I'll outline how I find this jumping-off point for all my decorating projects because, not to sound clichéd, but inspiration really is all around us. My goal is to guide you to peek inside a few new corners where you may not have thought to look before. My sources of inspiration keep me on my creative toes and are particularly helpful when I need to be rescued from a rut. In addition to sharing my approach, I'll also guide you through some proactive approaches for soaking up as much as possible in the least amount of time so that you can step away feeling refreshed and energized. You'll find lots of questions to answer, so pull out some paper for jotting down your thoughts and take advantage of the writing space on pages 21, 22 and 29 that have their own prompts for including personal musings – it's time to break a few rules here and write in a decorating book. So grab your pencil – this will be fun!

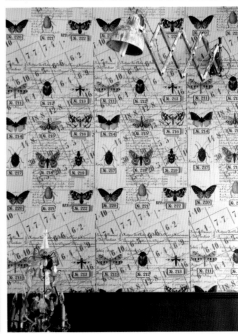

WHAT DO YOU LOVE?

List some things that you really, really love. They can range from your partner to your dog, the watch your mother gave you when you graduated, an award you've won, the smell of fresh cut grass, the bright red vintage vase your grandmother gave you . . . As you list everything, think about how you could better display or show you cherish and value these things in your home. In other words, if you truly love that red vase, why is it hidden in the china cabinet? Perhaps it should go in the glass display case instead?

LOOK OUTSIDE OF WHAT YOU CALL FAMILIAR

You never know what random bits may inspire a new room scheme or a single item in your home – perhaps a skirt you are drawn to will inspire new bedroom curtains. Think outside of the box because boxes are only created in our heads anyway – they don't really exist, we just put them there and inside stash away all that makes us comfortable. Once the box is removed, new things can flow freely in and out. Allow yourself a little creative room to explore and expand your views.

WHAT ARE YOUR 'SAFE' COLOURS?

Just for fun, examine the colours you surround yourself with at home and in your wardrobe. Consider what new ones you could add to the usual mix. Try experimenting with a touch of neon mixed with pastel, for instance. Think of colours you do not use that you want to experiment with. Grab some paint swatches so you can refer to them when we talk about colour later in the book.

WHAT IS YOUR IDEAL SCENT?

What are some of your favourite perfumes? When it comes to scented candles, which are your favourites and why? How do the scents that you love make you feel? How do you use them in your home? What do you smell when you enter your home and do you like it? How does this affect how you feel at home? Now that you know what you love to smell, think of ways to use scent at home to create a warm interior space. And remember, you don't want to mask a musty whiff with room spray so consider first getting to the root of the problem, removing it and then you can layer in your fragrant touches.

LIST THE FILM INTERIORS THAT YOU LOVE

What are some of your favourite film interiors? Do you tend to like a very modern, minimalistic scheme, an eclectic one, or maybe a smart urban loft? If you spot a theme in film interiors that speaks to you then consider what your findings reveal about your interior leanings, and consider how you can translate some of that into your home design.

WHAT ARE SOME OF YOUR FAVOURITE SONGS AND HOW DO THEY MAKE YOU FEEL?

Do you enjoy listening to music? What do you listen to at home? How does it make you feel? When you are at stores or restaurants, what songs do you respond to? I noticed that whenever I am shopping at Anthropologie I feel very upbeat and positive and realized it has to do with the music they play. Now I always ask what they have on and am introduced to new artists this way, but beyond that I make sure to add it to my playlist at home to enhance the overall mood. Where do you like to listen to music? If you enjoy relaxing in the tub to your favourite bands then you may want to invest in a small sound system for the bathroom. Music can be such a positive contribution to the overall spirit of a home.

HOMES OF FRIENDS

When you think of some of your friends' homes, which really stand out? How do you feel when you visit them? Does their personality shine throughout the home, does it feel personal? If so, try to examine how they are accomplishing this. Consider how you can take cues from what you love about these inspiring spaces that you can possibly apply to your own home.

LIST FIVE CITIES THAT YOU ADORE AND DETAIL WHY

Is it the culture? The food? The style? Architecture? A specific feeling? What can you learn about your favourite cities and how can you bring some of these special things into your life? If you have travelled to any of them maybe you could display a special treasure you found during your visit?

'I've added an eclectic mix of styles and finds both old and new in my living room to create a space that speaks to me. From my vintage patchwork rug purchased on a trip to Istanbul to art I've hung off-centre with felted beads, a paper grandfather clock and a strip of favourite wallpaper, I like the energy in this room. I feel both inspired and at peace here. '

THIS PAGE: I found the lampshade in the corner on eBay and decided to strip it down to its wire frame and then I wrapped it with fabric strips. Personalizing a room, even the slightest touch, goes a long way.

INSPIRING SPACES

It was love at first sight the moment I stepped into this charming Parisian apartment belonging to set designer and artistic director Jean-Christophe Aumas. I was inspired by his collection of books and magazines, along with vintage gold letters. When you visit a friend's home try to home in on what inspires you the most. When I returned from Paris, I decided to display some of my books laid open, versus closed. Little changes can make a difference and I've noticed my guests flipping through my books much more often as a result.

THIS PAGE: A bold navy blue wall with a lovely Jean Prouvé cabinet from Vitra adds instant impact while also complementing the nearby vintage sofa. Strong touches of yellow, red and green tones add vivid jolts of colour and the futuristic notes of the artwork bring in a touch of humour.

What are some places that you absolutely love?

Think about places that inspire you. What feelings do they evoke? Consider how you can translate those elements in your space. Perhaps you love Parisian cafés because they make you feel romantic? You may need to add romantic touches to your kitchen – a bud vase by the sink, elegant plates to eat from at breakfast, vintage linens on the table. Do you see where I'm going? Good. Now I'll walk you through some places that inspire me. Ready to explore?

➜ ART GALLERIES If you haven't spent a quiet morning or a leisurely afternoon in an art gallery lately, try to pencil in some time for this creative excursion. Most galleries specialize in specific subjects, such as ceramics, photography, sculpture and paintings, so take your pick and treat yourself to a day trip. Art exposes us to new visions outside our own world and it is an enriching exercise to experience how others interpret subjects. We can then step back inside our own head to explore their interpretations.

I find smaller art galleries incredibly inspiring since their collections are more defined. Often their rooms are a blank canvas and very spare in a calming palette – usually white walls and pale wooden floors. This minimalist, clutter-free space encourages thought. The spaces in which we find art can provide much decorating inspiration, leading you to learn more about your personal style and inner longings as to how you wish to live. The key is to stay open-minded, to tap into your feelings as you experience them, ask yourself a lot of questions and pay attention to the answers.

WHEN IT COMES TO EATING OUT

- List some of your favourite restaurants and cafés.

- Now think about your list. What is it exactly that you like about each place? The food, interior, service, lighting, vibe? Be very specific.

- Close your eyes. Imagine your perfect restaurant interior. Think of how it feels as you enter. Imagine the lighting (dim? candlelight? bright?) and hear the music. Do you smell the delicious aroma? Try to feel the overall mood of the space. Would you be surrounded by people or quiet and secluded? Open your eyes now to detail your findings on paper. See what this says about you and how you could bring this into your home.

- Look over your findings again and try to spot a theme, a red thread as I call it, that runs through each place, which connects them. Perhaps each place has a great energy, and is vibrant and noisy. Or perhaps the atmosphere is minimalist and contemporary. Try this and see what you come out with. It can be quite revealing!

- Think of less obvious ways to mirror what you love about your favourite eateries. Maybe a certain way of dressing a table is one you can try? Perhaps overhead lighting is flattering – can you install a dimmer switch in the dining room? Spend some time thinking about this. This is simply your way of getting in better touch with what you are responding to, so have fun with it.

➜ MUSEUMS Museums don't have to be boring or just day trips for children. I visit both permanent installations and travelling exhibitions regularly, especially in my local natural history museum because art, science, nature (even dead and stuffed!) never ceases to spark my imagination. What inspires you about museum visits? Usually, and oddly enough, taxidermy inspires me the most. I know, dead animals doesn't sound so delightful on paper. Yet they intrigue me because most have such lovely patterns and texture to admire. In display cases you can study them and admire their beauty. The same applies to birds and insects. Their details can range from intricate patterns on delicate wings to iridescent gem-like shells and richly coloured ornate feathers. Curated cabinets of often endless curiosities spark my imagination and open my mind.

→ CAFES AND RESTAURANTS We all have favourite places to eat, but think for a moment. Is it only the yummy food that draws you in or are you also responding to the atmosphere? For me, it's usually a combination of both. I'm the first to admit that the thrill of grabbing a falafel on the corner of a busy city street can be fun in its own right. But the places I seek out for a well-rounded sensory experience are ones that go the extra mile and provide the whole shebang, from the vibe to the food, service and atmosphere. What is the point of eating out otherwise? Most of us have access to great markets and a slew of cookbooks and can easily whip up delicious meals at home. The social aspect of eating out combined with a night off from washing your own dishes is a draw, but beyond that, I eat out to experience an environment that makes me feel like I'm doing something good for myself.

→ HOTELS I often find the best decorating ideas for the living room and bedroom in hotels. I have a favourite hotel in London because it is such a well-decorated cosy retreat that is in a tree-lined neighbourhood far from tour buses and T-shirt shops. When I'm there I am drawn to all of the little details about this place that I love so much, from a new candle scent that they may be burning in the lobby or a CD playing in the background. When you are at a hotel consider what works about the space and what you can take home in the form of a good idea. (I'm not suggesting the bath mat!) Perhaps it's

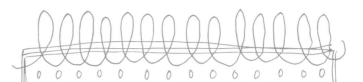

KEEPING A RECORD

An art gallery usually won't allow photography but you can sketch things that inspire you, purchase a postcard of the work if available or ask for a catalogue or the artists' websites so that you can stay connected to the work.

• • •

In most natural history museums you are allowed to take photos as long as your flash is turned off – but always ask first. Use this as an opportunity to practise your photography in often stunning buildings, while simultaneously snapping pictures of whatever catches your eye.

• • •

Other times I busily scribble down thoughts or sketch in my little notebook as visions pop into my head. A museum visit can also hint to some terrific display ideas for hanging art at home and give a fresh viewpoint for styling collections in cabinets or on tables. Often I bring a notepad, relax on a nearby bench and jot down my thoughts.

• • •

Keep your design antennae on. I took a photograph of white lacquered wainscot panelling paired with the most gorgeous robin's egg blue wallpaper recently in London, and that inspired the addition of blue in my guest bedroom. You never know where inspiration will strike and when it does, make sure to capture it on your camera.

the slate tiles in the bathroom, the hardware on the dresser drawer, the pattern of the duvet. Note what you are responding to and snap a photo or write it down in your travel notes.

→ OUTDOORS I have various private hideaways in my city where I escape to stroll, dream, observe and allow myself to be swept away in the moment of doing very little – which can feel great! Everyone has a different way to unwind; my way is to simply bring my camera and escape to a park, garden or in the forest behind my house. There I can use my imagination without interruption. I live in a vibrant city so I rely on these quiet zones to keep me grounded.

What do you enjoy reading?

Here are some must-reads that keep me on my creative toes, along with some tips on how I approach them. I encourage you to turn to books, magazines, e-mags, catalogues and blogs regularly, but particularly when you're in a rut.

→ BOOKS Decorating books are extremely helpful resources, but it's easy to become so swept away by pretty photos that you forget to read them. You don't want to miss out on gems of advice that you can apply to your project. Venture beyond interiors titles to include art, craft, flower arranging, fashion – even cookery books. Why? Because often you'll come across colour palettes, themes, shapes and textures that could be a real source of inspiration to you. Designers, stylists, artists, photographers and others who work in creative fields often provide alternative viewpoints that may be the fresh perspective you need. It is also common to become stuck in your own field of interest, since most people within certain fields are being inspired by the same things. It's all about casting a wide net to see what you can pull in.

→ MAGAZINES AND CATALOGUES These are a quick fix and you don't have to spend a lot of money on them or feel guilty about tearing out the pages. I am constantly marking up or tearing out pages that I like, posting them on my moodboard or filing them into my style files. Just like books, select from a variety of subjects and themes to stir your inspiration. Have you tapped into graphic design or baking magazines? How about gardening or architecture? You may be surprised by the amount of fresh ideas that you can gather.

In addition to trying out different topics, also check out magazines and catalogues from other countries. These are the most exciting and eye-opening creative resources for me. I started with British magazines when I was a teenager and today I have Danish, Japanese, Swedish, German, Dutch, Australian and so many other countries represented in my cabinet at home. Most major cities have international news stands where you can comb through gorgeous magazines, or you can subscribe to those that offer international subscriptions (though I must warn you this can be expensive so make sure that you really love them first). When it comes to catalogue do a little online research and locate brands that you love. You may not be able to understand the text but the eye candy can be quite yummy!

→ E-MAGAZINES In addition to the wild world of print there exists yet another fix called digital magazines, or e-magazines for short. Many are free to download or free to view online, and can be terrific resources to tap into for current viewpoints on everything from decorating to wedding planning and baking.

→ BLOGS A blog is a web log, or an online journal where people from all over the world share their thoughts in a way that works for them (text, video, imagery, etc.). While blog topics vary, the ones I read mostly fall into the topics of decorating, art, crafts, handmade, small business, creative writing, cooking, photography and other lifestyle themes that revolve around creative living. Most are authored by people I've never met, but through their writing and photography I can see that they are passionate and this can be very inspirational. With the growing popularity of decorating and design blogs worldwide there are many with intriguing viewpoints and imaginative bloggers, making it easy to slip into a creative rabbit hole for hours. I love blogs!

List your inspirations...

- My favourite places to visit and why . . .

- Other ways to gain inspiration are . . .

- When I'm in a creative rut, I seek out . . .

- Additional thoughts that I've learned so far . . .

21

What your magazine reading says about you

When magazines arrive on my doorstep, I instantly rip open their packaging to take in the visual poetry that often follows – words, layouts, imagery. Even the touch and smell of a magazine is an experience that carries me off to imaginary places. How do I use this as inspiration though, outside of being momentarily entertained while curled up in my chair? I find it fun to identify what features in magazines that I flip to first, because it always reveals things about myself and my interests that I find fascinating. Let's try this exercise out on you. Grab a pencil and get writing!

First, what are some magazines that totally rock your world? List them below and note why.

_____

_____

_____

_____

_____

Once you are flipping through the magazine, where do you usually pause, what do you find yourself actually reading or marking? Trend reports? Product reviews? Home tours? Something else? List what stops you in your tracks below.

_____

_____

_____

_____

_____

When you crack open a fresh copy, what do you look forward to learning or seeing the most? Why?

_____

_____

_____

_____

_____

_____

_____

_____

How does this relate to decorating and personal style? The more you home in on what you respond to the closer you come to identifying key interests – look at the pink box to see how to channel this into your decorating projects.

_____

_____

_____

_____

_____

_____

_____

_____

IF YOU LOVE TREND REPORTS . . .

then mix in affordable of-the-moment pieces to your decor a few times a year to satisfy your trendy sweet tooth – you obviously enjoy staying ahead of the pack.

. . .

IF YOU ENJOY READING REVIEWS . . .

you may be concerned about making the best purchases and perhaps second opinions help you along in the process. When shopping, take along a dear friend with great taste similar to yours who can provide helpful feedback. Find virtual friends by reading their stylish blogs! Often you can find honest opinions from bloggers whom you admire that can steer you towards great products. If you worry about making mistakes when it comes to big-ticket items, another option until you boost your design confidence is to hire a design consultant or decorator to give you some support and help you to make the best decision.

. . .

IF YOU LOVE HOME TOURS . . .

you seek out new ideas for your own decorating projects by seeing how others live. Obviously this inspires your own creativity. Use some Post-it notes and get specific about what exactly you love about the home (or dislike). Be as critical or gushy as you'd like, as long as it is honest. Dissecting information helps you notice patterns in your thinking that ultimately help you to define your style, so your home becomes a more authentic reflection of self.

. . .

TEST THE THEORY . . .

and next time you read a magazine, highlight what you found most inspirational and take some notes. Better yet, tear out what caught your eye and add it to a notebook with notes as to what you found interesting. Over a period of time, usually five to ten magazines in, you will spot specific themes in your thinking that will show your leanings towards specific colours, textures, trends, styles – go ahead, try it and see for yourself!

' The more you tune in, the more likely you are to come away with something, from a great idea to an improved mood because you gained a creative boost. '

'A vintage over-dyed Turkish rug in hot pink makes a dramatic design statement. Don't be afraid to introduce bold colour in a mostly neutral space – often this is exactly what the room needs to take it from simply attractive to hot, hot, hot!'

THIS PAGE: The desk area was created using glossy Ikea cabinets and a custom-made desktop, which coordinates with the 'Loop Stand Table', from HAY in Denmark. A natural wood task light by Muuto in Norway complements the dining chair legs. The drum shade, 'Lulu' by Frau Maier, is white with gold lining, bringing the warmth of the wooden floor upwards, while the neon pink cord from House Doctor lends a punchy accent coordinating with the rug. Thoughtful little details express a unique point-of-view.

ABOVE: I look forward to working each day in this cheery nook! I painted the recessed wall in Elephant's Breath, which is a delightfully subtle 'greige' from Farrow & Ball. To block the strong sunlight that generally pours in during the day I made café curtains from 100-year-old German linen found on eBay. The overhead MHY pendant from Muuto floats quietly above my space, its curves mimicking the alcove and window. Favourite artwork that I've collected throughout the years was intentionally placed off-centre to reduce visual distraction over my monitor – blank space helps me to think more clearly.

ABOVE RIGHT: A pair of floating picture ledges act as both storage and a rotating display space for favourite books, boxes I've made, ribbon spools and Japanese washi tape in every colour and pattern. I intentionally display the tape because it is too colourful and pretty to tuck away. When displaying favourite magazines, like these from Lines & Shapes, I will occasionally show their covers not just their spines because graphic covers such as these double as artwork.

MY INSPIRATIONS

When I first moved into my home and was faced with this large room, I felt both excited and a bit overwhelmed. What would I use it for and how would I fill it? One day I simply walked into the room and closed my eyes and imagined the space. I saw myself teaching, mingling with my students and entertaining my family and friends. I finally found my inspiration – trapped in my head! I immediately tapped into my style files, drew up a floor plan, shopped from other rooms in my home and began to carve out my new studio. Sometimes you simply need to close your eyes to tap into the inspirations you've collected through the years.

Where do you like to shop?

Shopping is my guilty pleasure; I'm addicted to the process of both discovering new stores and visiting old favourites that constantly dazzle me with updated displays and new merchandise. Have your decorating radar on when you shop and scan for ideas to kick-start your scheme. Your first mission is to locate that single source of inspiration – your jumping-off point that will guide your vision. It's time to hunt and gather!

→ STORES I jokingly refer to myself as every storeowner's nightmare because I simply must come into physical contact with whatever resonates with me – I touch nearly everything that comes into my line of vision. I'm very sensory and connect to things primarily through touch. As a result, I'm constantly examining objects – flipping them over, running my fingers along a smooth ceramic rim or a velvet pillow.

I'm also very aware of my surroundings. If the retail space doesn't inspire me, then beautiful products won't win my attention either. The experience of being immersed in the retail space is almost as important to me as discovering something interesting. If an interior lacks that special touch I rarely return. Music, lighting, scent, displays, how well things are curated, cohesion, the overall vibe, how the staff interacts with me and one another – everything matters.

A book shop is another type of retail space that I enjoy and is a place of contrasts – both peaceful and energizing, inspiring and overwhelming, reflective and a chance to escape reality. You can let your imagination run free, so make it a point to examine the many aisles.

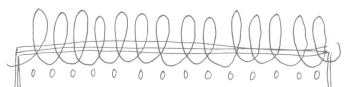

WHAT DOES YOUR SHOPPING BEHAVIOUR REVEAL?

What do you love about some of your favourite stores? What do you find yourself drawn towards when shopping – what kinds of products? Do you notice the interior of the space (ceiling details, wall treatments, flooring, windows) or do you tend to bypass that and pay more attention to the details in the visual displays – how items are stacked and presented on shelves, for example? Do you notice the music? How does it impact your overall experience?

• • •

Notice packaging on products. What appeals to you? Is there anything you could try at home? I once saw some fabric-wrapped soaps and, using scrap fabrics, I wrapped guest soaps using vintage fabric I had in my cabinet and left them in the guest bathroom stacked on a small shelf. The patterns made them look so much prettier.

• • •

Why do you love and feel inspired by your favourite book stores? When you shop next time, make it a point to visit sections that you usually pass by. For instance, browse young adult titles, children's books, travel, psychology, nature … You may stumble upon something that really strikes a chord. It can be the book cover, subject, illustrator, layout, photography – pay attention to what you are responding to.

' *Through shopping I learned something about myself – that I am tactile and crave texture in my surroundings. I love a variety of texture, from supple leathers to sumptuous woollen blankets. What do you respond to when you're out and about?* '

→ MARKETS AND FAIRS Who doesn't love strolling through an outdoor market on a sunny day? Whether you are looking for art, a handmade doll for your child, fresh fruit or antique furniture many of us seek out flea and farmers' markets and craft fairs that stock the things that we are looking for and, commonly, these markets are outdoors. The combination of sunshine, fresh air, lots of people, a delicious smell (like crêpes!) and shopping has to be one of my favourite sensory experiences. When I'm at an open air market I always bring my iPhone so I can take notes on it or snap photos of things that catch my eye. Be ready for an adventure!

WHEN IT COMES TO SHOPPING MARKETS

- Ask questions – don't be afraid to learn about the items that you see.

- Look for trends. What craft themes do you see? What are the changes in how dealers are displaying their wares? Do you see certain themes popping up again and again – such as industrial lighting or vintage bottles in blue and green tones? You may be onto something.

- Go for the first things that catch your eye and ask, 'Why am I responding to this?'

- Make it your mission to find a special item that you really connect with, rather than a bunch of little things that you simply like.

- View markets as a great way to travel the globe without leaving your city. Spanish olives, Moroccan blood oranges, vintage linen from Belgium, Canadian maple syrup . . . . this can be inspiring.

- Bring a mini moodboard with you (see details on page 127) to ensure you don't buy something that is 'off' colourwise or that may not fit into the dimensions of your space. It is so frustrating to make a purchase that doesn't fit into its intended space that you are unable to return, so arrive prepared for best results.

- BYOB . . . bring your own bags – sturdy ones!

- It's wonderful to bring along friends on market excursions, but be aware that those who share your taste, or are looking for a similar object, may present some challenges. You may want to agree to split up and meet back at a certain time to avoid having awkward moments when you both are hoping to own the same lovely pieces! If I am on a serious hunt for a specific project I tend to visit markets alone to limit distraction and so that I'm buying only what I love and not what my shopping companion thinks would work.

- Money talks! Always carry cash as most won't accept plastic.

- Take in the buzz. From vendors chatting with customers to the street musicians strumming away on their guitars, the sensory overload is both delightful and overwhelming.

- Know when to fold 'em . . . The moment when the exhilarating vibe of a market becomes too much, walk away. It is better to leave with a head full of ideas and positive memories. If you overstay your welcome you risk burn out and what fun is that? You really can have enough of a good thing.

List your favourite shops and markets

'These rooms show how a love for shopping at markets translates into an eclectic vibe at home. Great furniture from different eras and funky lighting pack plenty of wow factor. Make it your goal to locate special pieces that you'll adore for years to come.'

OPPOSITE: A complementary colour scheme in blue and orange is warm and masculine in this Parisian apartment owned by American stylist James Leland Day. A melange of old and new pieces along with carefully curated salon-style artwork lend character and bring the pattern upwards onto the walls while the bold blue wall provides the perfect background to showcase his favourite works.

THIS PAGE: Flea market finds from Belgium, France and beyond make for lovely display pieces assembled en masse. Vintage finds mix well with delicate porcelain tableware and cups in white from Astier de Villatte in Paris.

STEP 2 FIND YOUR PERSONAL STYLE

' Finding your personal style need not be tedious or labour intensive. In fact, I'd like to approach this step as casually as we possibly can. I'm not a fan of boxing in with a single style label, nor do I encourage anyone to decorate in a way that reflects a specific style more than their own personal style. '

There are some homes that I've visited where I instantly thought of a designer or look, not the personality of the homeowner. I'd like to steer you away from that. Finding your personal style is all about tapping in and considering the story that you want your home to tell about you, your family and your life. Perhaps what speaks to you is a mix of country with clean modern lines, some industrial elements and retro floral patterns. While this may appear unfocused you aren't as 'all over the place' as you may think. In fact, most people like many different things. It is not critical that you identify your personal style in a few words, you simply need to call out what you like. Once you determine for instance that you are 'Bohemian modern with a dash of romantic country, and a little bit vintage', you can begin curating what fits that style and then weave that into your vision for the space, so it begins to look and feel more personal to you. If you have your style files handy, try looking at them now and start labelling your tears with descriptive words that more closely define your style.

How do you express yourself?

We are each capable of creative thinking, some of us just need to give ourselves the permission to think more creatively and to not allow ourselves to be boxed in or limited by mental blocks. I'm sure that some of the writing prompts in this book so far have given you a gentle nudge in the right direction. We all need a friendly nudge and as your decorator friend I will cheer you on, I promise!

→ THERE ARE NO WRONG ANSWERS And there are few rules when it comes to creative expression. Please keep that in mind as you respond to the writing prompts throughout this book. Decorating guidelines exist because we need them. We can be creative on a hob with our meal preparation, yet we still need to follow some guidelines while cooking. We also need certain tools to perform specific tasks more easily – a hammer is meant to drive a nail into a wall, not the handle of a broom! The broom handle may work, but not as efficiently as a hammer. Decorating and creative self-expression in general may have some guidelines, but this framework is intended to make the process a bit easier, not to hold you back or constrain you in any way.

→ UNDERSTAND BASIC DESIGN PRINCIPLES This gives you a good foundation to build on, but from there the personality and beauty of the space is up to you. You are ultimately in charge of breathing life into your home and giving it character, soul, a vibe that is an honest reflection of what you and your family are all about. Only then can you begin to influence your space in a positive way so that you feed it, it feeds you. Through this symbiotic partnership you form with your home, you are able to feel nurtured, free, aware, loved and connected. Think back to a time when your interior space felt right. Maybe it was the entire home or just a room. Didn't it feel better coming home when you actually looked forward to being in the room?

→ HAVE CONFIDENCE IN YOUR CREATIVE EXPRESSION Give yourself the time and patience that you deserve to ask questions, build your confidence, test ideas and venture through this book, which is all about encouraging the exploratory process of learning more about who you are first so decorating becomes more natural and an extension of self. Plus, let's be really honest here – when it comes to decorating, what is there to really fear? In the end, your room is usually just four walls, a ceiling and a floor and will the world fall apart if your rug doesn't match your new wall colour? Not really. You may get irritated, but then you can move the rug to a new room and move on with plan B. You're inherently creative, you can do it!

→ DIG DEEP INSIDE YOURSELF This may at first feel odd if it doesn't come as second nature, but questioning why something rocks your world, then thinking of how to take certain elements of that into your home will become second nature the more you practise this way of looking at things. It's also how to make daily impressions matter – taking cues and translating them into ideas that inspire you in some way can add whole new meaning to what you thought was only mundane routine. The moment you hop out of the hamster wheel so many of us are running in each day and spend a little time exploring your surroundings you can find more pleasure and even peace. I believe peace of mind comes through many things, but nurturing ourselves and getting in touch with who we are at a core level, for me at least, is how I find this peace.

Who are you?

Where do you escape to, to tune in to what makes you, you? A little time out can definitely help you to tap into your creative side, too. When you're alone, capture your thoughts and feelings on this page. It may seem strange to find such questions in a decorating book, but I believe that the key to making your home inspirational to you is to figure yourself out and define your personal style first, then the other things will more naturally fall into place. Here are some ideas to think about to get you started:

What did you love to do as a child?

As an adult, what catches your eye today? Do you see any connections with what you loved as a child? Often you will see a direct connection, which can help you to remember who you are in case work and life in general have got in the way.

What did you want to be when you grew up?

What are your hobbies? What would you like to try?

What things caught your interest as a teenager?

What are some of your favourite things, from films to music?

PERSONALIZING YOUR HOME

Feeling comfortable with who you are and the decisions you make doesn't always come easily, does it? It takes considerable work for some people to feel at ease with who they are. I don't look at this as a problem though; we're only human and it's natural to be unsure at times. In many ways it's positive when you recognize your insecurities may be holding you back, because only then can you begin to make productive changes. I've had ups and downs in my life and noticed that when I wasn't feeling good in my own skin my home reflected my insecurity and was a bit bland and 'safe'. When I started feeling at peace again my home environment evolved in a

positive way too. While this isn't a self-help book by any means, 'therapist' is often a role decorators and designers take on when working with clients – analyzing not only the space but also those living there. Designers have to dig deep and get into their clients' heads to help them tap into their true style. It makes sense. It's time to get real and connect our vision of how we want to live with the reality of how we are living. Carve out some quiet time to reflect how you can bring more of your heart and soul into your living space. The only approval needed is from you, so say yes more to your decorating ideas and create a home that resonates with you.

' Your home should reflect the story of your life and be filled with things that you feel a connection to, whether it is a memory, a mood, your values or how you wish to become in the future. There is nothing wrong with making your home reflect the person that you were, are and hope to be. '

OPPOSITE: This bedroom dresser top has an eclectic mix of engaging treasures that I had fun examining while in the country home of English photographer Emma Lee. In addition to the few objects already on display, I gathered others from the bedroom that I felt oozed Emma's personal style and grouped them here. I'm not sure who the baby is, but adding it definitely brought in a personal touch, along with the little shoes and the painting, which I think goes so nicely with the dried craspedia flowers in the vase.

ABOVE LEFT: When we were shooting in Paris I fell in love with the apartment of American stylist James Leland Day. James possesses glorious style that he seems to effortlessly breathe into his space. It is his creative canvas, and constantly evolves with his taste. James is a lover of creating finishing touches through colour, pattern, whimsical objects and well-edited collections with tons of character. This vignette in his dining room is very James. When you look at the vignettes in your own home, are they so very you?

ABOVE: Isn't this a pretty set of objects? Originally only the lamp and glove form sat side-by-side on this cabinet top, but to enhance the already personal vibe I decided to show you some of my favourites from this home by adding in some flowers, vintage jugs and yarn. This is a great tip if you are looking to add personality to your home. Namely, think of the story that you are trying to tell through your objects. What do you wish to communicate? How can your objects make that story come alive and have greater meaning to you?

The southwest London home of French jewellery designer Emma Cassi is so stylish, classic, personal and cosy, don't you think? It's also very approachable. In her own work, Emma displays the touch of an artisan to create an exquisite collection blending traditional craft with a modern twist, giving her designs timeless appeal. In her home, she has applied the same feminine touch with texture and colour that I love so much. A neutral foundation allows her some flexibility for moments when she's gravitating towards a certain colour, trend or style – she can simply add or take away cusions and throws or rearrange her built-in storage or fireplace mantel, which is a great decorating tip for those who like to change things up frequently without investing in a total overhaul.

'Jewellery designer Emma Cassi mixes and matches styles and periods according to whatever calls out to her, almost effortlessly putting everything in place. Her home reflects her work, which in turn reflects her personality.'

ABOVE: After visiting Emma's home I collected a few things around my own home to show you how I would interpret Emma's style while staying true to my own voice and style. When you find a home in a magazine that inspires you, try grouping things on the table that you think tell your story while also pulling out key elements from the photo that resonate with you. From there, you can begin to build a more definite idea of how you envision your room, but for now this is a great start and gets you in the right head space to build your idea further and make it your own.

OPPOSITE: The chromatic unity of this space in its mostly all-white scheme provides the perfect canvas for decorating. In order to break up the white space Designer's Guild 'Wharton Black & White' wallpaper in hand-drawn floral patterns was added behind the sofa. White wooden floors are topped with a warm beige carpet, adding a cosy touch and a more natural element so that the room doesn't appear cold. The warm patina of the vintage leather chest lends warmth and it is reinvented as both storage and a coffee table.

How do I get confident with colour?

One of the most personal choices you make is the selection of colour. Colour has character and gives a space life, individuality and style. It can calm, energize, motivate and inspire. Whether used in small doses or in large over-the-top displays, colour has confidence. You can use it to create harmony or tension, to conceal areas of a room or to punctuate others. Colour can make a space come together beautifully.

➔ HAVE NO FEAR The keys to decorating with colour are to be fearless and confident. Our level of self-confidence can show in many ways and influences nearly every aspect of our lives, including how we decorate. Experimenting with colour need not evoke fear and trembling; after all this is only decorating – world peace is not at stake! Some avoid colour because they think they'll mess up, doubting their ability to pull it together effectively. Do you have fear? Why?

➔ TRUST YOUR VISION Creating with colour comes down to taking risks and relying on your gut instinct. For some, working with it seems very natural and for others learning basic colour theory can help lay a solid foundation first. I learned colour theory in design school but when I decorate today the colour wheel is exchanged for simply allowing my eye and instinct to guide my decision-making. In other words, I don't sweat it.

➔ PLUNGE IN AND ENJOY Let me reassure you that you're not being tested or judged, this is your home and practising in your personal space is the best place for building skill and

SOME THINGS ABOUT COLOUR THAT ARE HELPFUL TO KNOW . . .

VALUE: The lightness or darkness of a colour.
INTENSITY: The brightness or dullness.

HUE
Definition: Another name for colour. Hue is also referred to as pure colour. Red, orange, yellow, green, blue and violet.
Characteristics: Happy, bold, bright.
Ideal spaces: Classrooms, playrooms, kids' rooms, offices and kitchens.

SHADE
Definition: Created by adding black to a pure colour to reuce lightness. Maroon, navy, emerald.
Characteristics: Moody, mysterious, deep.
Ideal spaces: Dining rooms, bedrooms, offices and living rooms.

TINT
Definition: Created by adding white to any pure colour to increase lightness; can also be referred to as a pastel. Pink, light blue, mint green.
Characteristics: Romantic, feminine, soft.
Ideal spaces: Bedrooms, bathrooms, living rooms and sunporches.

TONE
Definition: Created by adding grey to any pure colour to make it duller than the original. Sage green, burnt orange.
Characteristics: Sophisticated, modern.
Ideal spaces: All spaces.

confidence. In fact, the more you practise the better you'll become. Don't be afraid of colour – often the best decorating idea comes from buying the wrong colour of paint! When we begin to see progress and reach goals our confidence grows alongside our skill level so practise, practise, practise and indulge a little!

How does colour make you feel?

We think we know what we like, but are you in touch with the physical effects that colour has on you? Think about how colour affects your mood, for instance. Saturated colour like pure red stresses me out completely if used in large doses, while tints, tones and shades of red suit me just fine. If I do use pure red, I like to tone it down by pairing it with cool blue.

How do the colours that you tend to gravitate towards make you feel?

Think about where you might use those colours. If blue gives you a sense of rest, for example, try using it in the bedroom. If yellow makes you feel energetic, it may be a nice accent for the office. Your reactions to colour may not necessarily be tied to scientific findings, either. What may evoke calm in one person may irritate another.

NATURALLY NEUTRAL

Neutral nesting need not be boring. In fact, sometimes less is more if you work with your subdued palette using intuition and a sensitive eye. Neutral rooms can range from the modern grey country cottage with subtle notes of accent colours, such as goldenrod and sage, to a slick city apartment with a mostly cream palette, ebony-stained wooden floors and a supple brown leather Chesterfield sofa for contrast. You can even go a bit dramatic with a more Scandinavian-inspired black-and-white scheme or try an all-white contemporary look in a loft space.

Consider the details – this is especially critical when dealing with neutrals, because they can so easily turn drab or dated. What are some ways to make neutral spaces stand out by being subtle? First, mix your neutrals. This keeps things interesting, so try combining beige and cream, black with grey, beige and white, or even several different tones of white with a hint of black. Finally, don't forget texture. Oh my goodness, this is important! A cowhide rug, wood flooring, metallic leather cushions, rattan chairs, a cable knit throw, silk shantung curtains – all can make a huge difference since they'll add warmth and life, inviting you to sit down and chill in your naturally neutral zen den.

ABOVE: The light and airy monochromatic scheme in the home of blogger and stylist Desiree Groenendal in Amsterdam is harmonious and laid-back, with a touch of rocker chic. I felt so at ease in her space because everything was so well considered but also very budget-friendly. Her low white cabinet is from Ikea, but when topped with white-washed wood panels from a home store that she simply laid on top it suddenly looks custom-made, warm and personal. Framing rock posters and favourite photography in graphic black frames and leaning them against the wall is a terrific decorating idea if you like to frequently change your displays.

OPPOSITE: The calm palette in this bedroom is so inviting. For me, the layers of texture in this limited colour palette is what keeps it alive and interesting. Pale mint, rose and yellow combined with beautiful materials gives this room a luxurious and comfortable vibe. When you work with neutrals, pay special attention to layering in a variety of materials and textures to add character, from embroidery to leather, ceramics, stitch-work, delicate trims, lace, crochet, straw, wool, metal, linen and wood. Try to stick with three core colours and mix and match them throughout the space.

A NEUTRAL BASE

Neutrals can be a terrific foundation to build from or the inspiration for an entire room scheme – it really comes down to how you use them. Organic neutrals can be intimate, soothing and inviting, while the more graphic pairings, such as black and white, can be bold and powerful. A key trick to keep in mind is to consider the amount of natural light you have and the undertones in your shades, because not all whites are created equal. Some whites have a warm, almost yellow, undertone while others have a cooler, bluish tint. A good rule of thumb is that if your room is a bit dark, look for neutrals with warm undertones. If it is sunny, opt for those with cool undertones.

ABOVE: This inspirational grouping of objects was gathered after I styled the room on the opposite page, belonging to photographer Emma Lee. Inspired by her neutral interior, I went home and gathered things that reminded me of her space but that also reflected my own story and personality. This is a fun exercise to try at home when you find a room that speaks to you. Using the image as a guide, gather your inspirations together. It not only trains your eye and builds decorating confidence, but it could lead to a new room.

OPPOSITE: This neutral living room works because it has layers of texture to add warmth, a touch of pattern for visual interest and a well-curated display of sentimental objects that tell a story. I love how they are presented in a simple, horizontal row, too.

ADDING TEXTURE AND TONE

Consider layering neutrals in different tones because if you're working with mostly white in the same tone you may end up with a dental office versus a home office. You may want to look for ways to allow in more natural light to eliminate shady corners or dark hallways, where a neutral space can appear drab or even dirty. Utilize as much natural light as possible if you're going for a light and bright look. You can try the quick and budget-friendly version by using mirrors to bounce light and simple sheers for window treatments or, if you can afford it and the architect gives you the go ahead, install transom windows above interior doors so light can flow more freely throughout your home. If your goal, however, is to create a modern, edgy space, then natural light may not be a concern. You might want a moody, dramatic space where shadows only serve to enhance the look.

Another detail not to miss when working with neutrals is to work in some pattern. A little animal print, bold stripes, petite polka dots, any and all patterns can add personality and style. And inject lots of texture in the mix, in the form of rattan, wood, stone, fur, leather – whatever you want!

' Combine neutrals with other neutrals. Mix various tints, shades and tones to add depth and contrast. And it's okay to cheat a little! Subtle notes of accent colour can be a refreshing change, and remember that a litle pattern adds personality so go for it. It's your house! '

FAR LEFT: A touch of mint green, buttery yellow and chocolate brown in this mostly neutral Dutch living room provides colour and contrast, life and personality. Whimsical patterns are combined with florals, plains and more graphic cushions, giving the overall space a sense of humour, which is reflective of the homeowner, stylist Tinta Luhrman, who has a bright, playful spirit herself and a very happy, energetic baby. Neutrals can be fun, too! She was careful not to let her mostly neutral palette become too grown up or serious so she has many handmade elements and a good mix of old and new furniture to make it approachable, liveable and balanced.

CENTRE: Layers of cushions, mismatched dining room chairs, a simple wooden bench as a coffee table, favourite things grouped on shelves, a pair of mint green pendant lights (a favourite design element of the space according to Tinta), a single wall painted in warm yellow – these rooms work because the flooring, palette and overall vibe is harmonious, unifying the space and making it feel more spacious. With the doors removed between the dining and living area, the current open floor plan allows in more natural light and makes entertaining a breeze.

ABOVE: Add a personal, unique stamp! This Dutch home had bare concrete walls that the homeowner opted to leave partially exposed when she discovered them during a renovation. After taping off a space to ensure clean, straight lines, the walls were painted white, leaving the taped-off rectangle in gorgeous, decorative raw concrete in this unusual space.

FABULOUS FURNITURE

The process of identifying the right furnishings can be a lot of fun if you start to look at furniture as more than simply functional – it can be decorative, too. Whether you choose to add a piece as a focal point or an accent, you can do so much with furniture so consider choosing pieces that really speak to you in order to elevate your room from good to great. There are thousands of terrific pieces to choose from, including those that you can customize with paint, fabric, new hardware, trim or stylized legs. With so much choice, it's essential to really identify the look you want to bring in and find pieces that help you to achieve that.

ABOVE LEFT: In this kids' room there are many good ideas to consider. I like the hook hung at kids' level since it encourages little ones to be tidy, while a petite stool provides the perfect spot to tie shoes. Painting a vintage dresser in a soft neutral tone like the lovely grey shown adds fresh new life while making it easier to move into other parts of the home should the child outgrow it – no need to repaint since this colour works in nearly any space.

ABOVE: Soften a more formal sofa by adding a few comfortable cushions for seating on top. These striped cushions soften the look of the sofa, making it more inviting to lounge upon. The sofa is not placed directly beneath the mirror, which is a refreshing change as so often we strive for perfect symmetry and this can frankly be boring! Its off-centre placement adds interest while the single soft blue cushion gives the predominant neutrals a lift.

THIS PAGE: This neutral space is warm and inviting, especially with those high-gloss wood floors that are both rustic and sophisticated. In fact, those floors were the first thing I noticed (and loved) when I stepped into this Brooklyn brownstone. All eyes are on the floors but you can't miss the ornate fireplace and complementary mirror that is situated between the front windows along with the gorgeous chandelier overhead. It's glam while also being a bit understated, don't you think?

MIX IN SOME COLOUR

It's easy to assume everyone loves colour and is comfortable using it but we're the oddball who has a tough time with it. Not the case! Colour can be a love/hate relationship for many. On one hand, we love it – it makes us happy, it evokes a certain feeling. On the flipside, we may fear it, lacking confidence and reasoning that since it doesn't come naturally it's best to avoid it and live in a beige world. That's fine if you genuinely connect with neutrals – there are plenty of confident decorators out there who surround themselves with black and white, because they prefer not to use colour.

In my own home shown, I've added various hues, mostly through accessories. This isn't because colour freaks me out – I like to switch things up frequently so keeping the foundation neutral in white, grey and wood tones gives me the flexibility I need to play with the layers on top and this often includes experimenting with playful hues as the mood strikes.

FAR LEFT: My towering grey bookcase was once natural wood but I decided to paint it grey to enhance its size and to provide a moody backdrop for my favourite books. The tiny stool is so out of scale but I love it there. Things don't always have to make sense or be 'by the book'; as long as it makes sense to you then it works!

CENTRE: Bringing in colour through plates on the wall works well above this streamlined white storage cabinet in my living room. Each plate has special meaning to me; two are from a trip to Turkey and the third, a John Derian moth plate, is from Astier de Villatte in Paris. I picked it up while we were shooting the shop for this book. Beyond aesthetics, it makes my heart happy to see these plates. That is my goal when I display things – to conjure up positive thoughts.

ABOVE: I painted the doors of this 100-year-old dresser using Farrow & Ball paint – I mixed 'Arsenic' and 'Churlish Green' and decided to have some fun one afternoon. The colours pull in some green from my mid-century Cherner chair, upholstered in Amy Butler's Primrose fabric in aqua from her Nigella collection. I transformed an old drawer by lining it with a pretty paper and installing it on the wall. I now use it to display favourite things and small pieces of art that I collect.

' Colour blocking is in vogue on the catwalk and at home. In fact, bold statement-making colour combinations look confident and alive. If you are feeling particularly daring, pastels and primary hues can be mixed for a dynamic, unexpected twist. '

OPPOSITE: When trying this look at home, ground the room in a neutral, then work your colour-blocking magic from there. For instance, pair solid complementary colours from the same family on the colour wheel to create harmony in your interiors. Royal blue and turquoise work nicely together, for instance. When working with cool tones, try to keep cools together. The same advice applies to warm colours such as red, orange and yellow. Black, royal blue, yellow and rosebud pink, as shown in the

Parisian apartment of Voici-Voilà art director, Jean-Christophe Aumas, is loud and proud. I love this look. If you want to go the extra mile, mix neons with earth tones or combine contrasting jewel tones. Talk about colour confidence!

ABOVE AND ABOVE LEFT: When applying colour to your walls, get creative! No need to simply paint them from floor to ceiling in the traditional sense. Try taping off sections, add your own decorative motifs like triangles or pinstripe borders, even paint the inside of doorways for drama. Study the details in this living room and notice how the black line continues around the top of the room, and how the pink wall is trimmed with a slim yellow border. Be daring, it's your home!

OPPOSITE: In the dining room of James Leland Day's apartment, his salon-style art grouping makes for a gorgeous focal point against a deep blue wall. James opted to use a strong ground colour on a single wall to provide a stunning backdrop for the artwork, making it really stand out. While many shy away from using bold, rich colour in small rooms, thinking it makes a room feel smaller, a trick of the trade is to avoid encapsulating colour by simply adding your intense hue to a single wall. Charcoal, indigo blue, crimson, goldenrod . . . all can stand in stark relief to surrounding white walls and pale wooden floors.

THIS PAGE: Here James Leland Day uses bold colour on his signature feature wall behind the bed in a luscious saffron yellow. The Danish mid-century cabinet grounds the space in warm brown. The bold botanical German school chart on the wall along with artwork leaning on the cabinet really stands out against the walls, adding a very graphic finishing touch that works in this space. Imagine if this wall were white? It wouldn't be the same room. Colour is your friend, so experiment!

COLOUR SHOTS

If you are uncertain about introducing strong colour you could start off small-scale with the furniture. Try painting an old cabinet and then placing it in the room. If you don't like it you can always try again with a different shade. Or even ring the changes once in a while by repainting it to see where that leads you – you might be inspired to create a whole new colour scheme for the entire room.

'*Small flashes of strong colour can really lift a space and change the mood dramatically. Using individual items of furniture is a great way of doing this as you can move them around easily.*'

FAR LEFT: Recognized as a stimulant, red encourages action and confidence while also increasing enthusiasm, so it's a good choice in a home office. This space showcases primary red as the dominant accent colour to add a whimsical, youthful spirit so the space isn't overly serious or stuffy. I love how red is kept in three key aesthetic places; the task chair, desk lamp and the wall organizer are set low, middle and high.

CENTRE: A simple wooden cabinet painted blue brings a little colour pop to this Brooklyn kitchen/dining room combo. Blue is a nice hue for a dining room because it causes the body to produce chemicals that calm the spirit, and what better way to feel than calm during dinner or in the morning while enjoying the newspaper and a cup of coffee?

ABOVE: The moment I entered the hallway of this English home in the countryside I spotted this fun yellow chair and thought that this was truly a clever addition the homeowner made to the space. Yellow tends to advance from surrounding colours and sparks creativity, plus it has vibrance and adds so much life. A simple chair in the right colour can really make a space!

' I like to play around and experiment when I'm missing colours I imagine would work. I pull from my fabric piles or my paint swatch collection. A colour story can be a collection of crafty bits – buttons, threads, patterned tapes, paper – or it can be larger in scale – a dress, vintage flower, some wallpaper, a piece of artwork. '

CREATE COLOUR STORIES

Working on colour stories can be such a motivator. Specific colours that you don't currently use at home (maybe lemon yellow? or indigo blue?) may evoke a surprising and positive emotional response, and can lead to the perfect palette for your new guest bedroom perhaps. You won't know until you try. And you don't have to paint an entire room lemon yellow to know if you will like it or not. Begin small to explore your colour options. Try creating a vignette at home on a little shelf, on a table, inside a bookcase. Look around your home and either collect objects in a single colour family (blue) or palette (blue, yellow and green) or simply pick up whatever you love and sort them by palette on your tabletop.

ABOVE LEFT: Blue and grey with touches of green make this dining area both warm and inviting. Used together, they form an analogous colour scheme, which means that on the colour wheel these hues sit together. They tend to create comfortable and serene settings because they are harmonious and are often found in nature, making them pleasing to the eye. A good tip when working with analogous colours is to choose one colour that dominates the scheme, along with one supporting colour and a third to bring in as your accent. Here, blue is dominant, the supporting colour is grey and the accent is green.

ABOVE: In this guest bedroom in Manhattan the homeowner uses a triadic colour scheme, which uses colours that are evenly spaced around the colour wheel, to bring life to a mostly neutral space. Red, yellow and a touch of blue add vibrance, personality and fun. To use a triadic scheme successfully, though, you need to exercise balance so a single colour should dominate, in this case yellow, while the other two act as accents. By the way, isn't that bedding so pretty? I love the whole ethnic modern vibe going on there . . .

THIS PAGE: Serene and lovely, this corner nook in Brooklyn uses cool tones of blue and violet with flecks of green to create a zen-like feel. With its analogous colour scheme, everything about this corner feels right – the blue vintage bench as a coffee table, the colour-washed pillow, the ornate birdcage and the fluffy pastel-toned rug all make for a well-balanced and harmonious display. Not too much, not too little – just right.

INJECT SOME COLOUR IN YOUR HOME

A bright throw on the sofa, bold artwork, stacked cushions on the floor, books on a shelf, an array of ceramic or glass vases – there are lots of ways to brighten up your home. Work with colour combinations that you respond to and you'll always be happy.

FURNITURE FUN

Paint an old cabinet in a bright colour. Apply wallpaper or paint on the inside of cabinets and drawers for a jolt of colour every time you open them.

STRONG COLOURS ON WALLS WILL ADD PUNCH

If you want to tame things down, paint only one wall or a defined part of a room, like the alcove.

FOR COLOURFUL KITCHENS

Add colourful hardware to cabinets. Choose from a range of brightly toned appliances, including hot neons. Add personality to open shelves with patterned porcelain china. Display food that has pretty packaging or pour sweets into glass jars.

lighting can add colour too

Look for drum shades as pendants with pattern and colour or pair simple white or black pendants with a colourful cord.

IN THE BEDROOM

Cushions, quilts, blankets, scarves and fabric pieces can dress up a bed. Use wallpaper as a headboard to add colour and pattern to a bedroom (see page 177 for a fantastic example). Add colourful trim to neutral curtains or paint your curtain rods turquoise, bold pink or sunny yellow.

EMBRACE THE HAPPY ACCIDENTS

Sometimes the wall colour may look better on a piece of furniture, so paint the table instead and find a different colour for the walls.

FLOWER POWER

Flowers used as brightly coloured graphic motifs on pillows and throws add a happy mood. And, of course, a selection of real flowers in vases always makes a delightful statement and lifts the room.

RECYCLE YOUR MAGAZINES

Work in some colour in a budget-friendly way by using some of your favourite magazines. In my sitting area (see page 23) I cut out pages collected from my magazine stash and arranged them into rows on my wall above the sofa. It added an instant focal point and colour pick-me-up. On a whim I can swap out my inspirations and change up my colour scheme, too.

DON'T FORGET FLOORS AND CEILINGS

Carpets, a selection of throw rugs, painted wooden floors, tiles – look for ways to introduce colour to your floors. Look upwards, too. Don't be afraid to ditch the safe white paint on the ceiling. Bright paint is an affordable way to add drama to a room, so go bold with a powerful statement shade. Or be subtle, with a variation on the wall paint.

What are your favourite colour tips?

Tear out four or five rooms with colours you love from your favourite magazines and create a collage of them on a sheet of paper using scissors and a simple glue stick. Jot down here all of your thoughts on why these rooms work, why you respond to the colours and which ideas you especially like. List the things you can take away and apply in your own home.

STEP 3 IDENTIFY YOUR PROJECT

‘ *Whether you wish to reupholster a set of unloved chairs, change your worktop or decorate your brand-new home from scratch, it's important that you identify your project first so that you can begin to focus and then channel your ideas into it, making that single project your primary concern.* ’

Have you ever noticed that if you don't get specific up front you tend to lose interest in a project and drop it midway? For instance, you may sense something in your home doesn't feel right anymore so you start shopping and adding to your home thinking that will help, but that only covers the problem and makes it worse. When you sense something isn't working, try to pinpoint the exact problem. I encourage you to take a clipboard and pen around your home and assess each room. Jot down what works and what doesn't work. See which room is begging for help or determine the nagging problem spot that is bringing down the room. Maybe your fireplace surround is the bad guy and could use a fresh update. In this step, you'll be encouraged to target the room or project by considering your starting point, building a timeline, the evil 'B' word (budget) and how to really carve out how you'll use the space. My goal is to put you in control so you are aware of what isn't working and can jump in with your decorator's cape on and save the day!

Where are you going to start?

When you are deciding where to apply your efforts first, examine your home and choose the room that screams the loudest. Figure out why it's broken and try to fix it. Here are some questions to get you started and plenty of space for you to pull together your thoughts.

If you're moving into a new home or building an addition apply these questions to individual rooms. This is an important step whether you are decorating a new space from scratch or for rooms simply in need of some sprucing up.

ASK YOURSELF . . .

- Which room in your home really needs your attention first?

- Why?

- What is the room currently being used for? Think about all activities.

- What would you prefer to use it as?
  For example: Is it a formal dining room that you never use? Would it be better used as a home office?

- What does your family use the room for?

- Do you need to incorporate their needs into your new room scheme?

- If so, how can you do that while still making the room fit your needs?
  For example: Include a nook for your daughter to colour and play as you work in your new office.

- What are some words that come to mind when you walk into the room currently?

- How do you feel in the room as it is now?

- What words and feelings would you rather associate to this space?

- What works currently in the space?
  For example: The fireplace surround is beautiful, you have great floors and good natural light.

- What doesn't work?
  For example: Your dainty chairs make your guests feel uncomfortable and your table is too small to fit everyone.

- What are some items that you'd like to keep in the room?

- What would you rather use in another room instead?

- What would you like to repurpose into something else?
  For example: Curtain fabric could be made into throw cushions.

- What would you like to keep in the room but alter to freshen it up?
  For example: New upholstery on a side chair.

- What story do you want the room to tell about your life and family?

- What personality traits do you recognize in yourself that you would want to share through your room scheme?
  For example: Are you vibrant, warm and creative? Social, down-to-earth and adventuresome? Bold, fashion-obsessed and urban?

- How do you imagine bringing some of those traits into your room?
  For example: If you are warm by nature, perhaps you could consider using your favourite colours to create a warm and welcoming atmosphere.

How big is your project?

How many times have you started a project, only to feel frustrated a few weeks later because you've realized that it was a much larger job than anticipated? Oh yes, I've been there, done that! There is nothing more likely to zap your zeal and threaten your resolve than a seemingly never-ending decorating project.

That is why it's critical to consider the scale of your project at the outset, and the many things that feed into making your idea a reality. Are you overhauling your bathroom? That's a big one that will take months of planning. Perhaps you've decided to add wainscot panelling to your en-suite bedroom? That can be another biggie, but not nearly as involved as a new bathroom. Maybe your project is small – you simply want to replace your bathroom sink, add a new shower curtain and paint the walls. I find that the best motivation when embarking on a decorating task is to list everything and tick items off as you go, no matter how big or small the project.

TIMELINE

When I was planning space and organizing moves as a project manager my job was to create elaborate spreadsheets that outlined every single step along the way. No stone was left unturned. As a result, work was completed on time and stress levels weren't soaring off the charts. I apply this to all of my decorating projects and I encourage you to do the same. Make sure that you are organized by planning out your project, considering all of the steps along the way. Create a timeline so that you can put your plans into action and work out all of the details, no matter what size your project is. Committing every detail to paper will move you towards the finish line in good spirits.

OPPOSITE: This built-in wall unit would be considered a medium-scale project. While it may seem small, you'll have several dependencies that need to be tapped into in order to bring this idea to fruition. You'll need to measure the space, decide how you want it to work and look (which may mean hiring a planner or architect to draw up detailed plans), then you'll have to hire a carpenter, call in an electrician to install your sockets and built-in task lighting, select the right paint colour, then paint the unit and finally decide on storage ideas, arrangement and seating. It's critical that you consider every piece in the puzzle before you tackle any project.

TOP RIGHT: Perhaps your project only consists of adding pendant lights to your dining room or you've decided to try the mismatched look around the table with a variety of chairs. For this, you'll need to map out the colours you'd like, the style of chairs you seek and whether you want one pendant or two. You won't need an elaborate spreadsheet, but lighting and furniture take time to acquire.

RIGHT: Wainscot panelling is the hallmark of a fine home and you may decide to install it in a few of your own rooms. For this project, you'll have many steps to consider along the way and will most likely need to hire help of various sorts so, again, planning is crucial.

What about the money?

Before proceeding with your decorating project, there is an elephant in the room that needs to be addressed. Your budget. This is often where we freeze in our tracks because what we want and what we can realistically afford is always a source of stress, isn't it? Why can't we all just be fantastically rich so we can buy whatever our heart desires?

I've seen homes belonging to celebrities, and while they have gorgeous things I find the best homes are ones where the homeowner had to tap into his or her creativity and rely less on buying what's already out there and more on creating something new – painting a dresser, adding different hardware to a cabinet, lining drawers with gorgeous wallpaper, painting floorboards in a favourite colour, dressing a window with handmade curtains embellished with a favourite trimwork. These personal touches give a home heart and soul and in most cases are not expensive. Their worth far outweighs their cost, and in such a commercial world isn't that refreshing?

While decorating an entire home at once or moving from a smaller home into a bigger one requires a larger budget than simply redecorating your living room, setting a budget is still required because only from there can you can determine what you can choose from to fit your budget. You will be redecorating rooms in your home many times in your life, so your only concern is telling your unique story through your interior as it is today. Approach your budget with the same open-minded flexible approach, and don't be afraid to get creative, take a few risks, ask for help, shop around, save up for splurge purchases and never say forever when it comes to any purchase. Doesn't that take some of the stress out of the equation?

WHAT'S YOUR SITUATION?

- You're decorating a new home from scratch.

- You need to decorate an empty room in your home that until now hasn't served much of a purpose. Perhaps it was just used as a storage area, or maybe it was a room belonging to a child who has moved out.

- You would like to redecorate a room (or several) in your home because the decor feels dated or no longer 'you'.

- You want to redecorate the entire home because you feel ready and need a change.

- You recently had to downsize, moving from a larger space into a smaller one.

- You recently moved from a smaller home to a much larger one and don't have enough pieces to fill it.

- You share space with someone that you are not related to (a roommate, dorm, etc.)

- You don't need to redecorate an entire room, but you are looking for ideas to freshen it up.

' *I'm a lover of handmade wares, custom-made pieces, original artwork and design classics, from lighting to furniture and beyond, but I cannot afford a home filled with these things. And yet it's having just a few of those very special pieces included in a space that often makes the biggest impact.* '

WHEN TO INVEST?

One of the biggest concerns people have is how to know if something is worth the investment. In the end, buy the best quality that you can afford and don't settle for something just because it's cheap. In a world of knock-offs and big box shopping, we can let price dictate what we ultimately purchase. Most of us see something we like and immediately flip it over to see how much it costs – it's only natural!

For some things, like a shower curtain, you don't need to be as concerned about quality because for the most part, shower curtains are what they are – pieces of fabric or plastic with holes along the top for rings, nothing more. However, when you shop for linens you need to consider purchasing the best quality you can afford. Things that you use daily will have a direct effect on how you feel. The big fluffy towels that give me a cosy hug after my daily bath make me feel good. The French hand soap in its pretty glass bottle on my sink is more expensive than that offered in the supermarket, but since I look at it regularly and it makes my hands look and feel better, I don't mind the small investment.

The same goes for furniture, textiles, flooring and other materials that we need for our homes. A piece of furniture that was handcrafted will be more expensive, but if it was made using the best-quality materials and laboured over by a pro it is more likely to be worth the investment. If you purchase something from an antiques dealer or high-end designer you can also expect to pay more. This isn't always because the quality is better (in some cases the quality isn't superior to similar pieces on the market) but they may prove to be a good investment. Whenever I try to purchase mid-century design classics on a site such as eBay, I notice that classic originals are highly sought after. There are other things that will cost more if it is handmade or an original, like artwork. An artist can spend days or weeks on a single painting. You have to consider that you are paying for the artistry – the talent and skill that went into creating the piece, along with the time and energy that they spent conceiving it and creating it. The same goes when shopping at

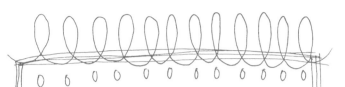

TO SPLURGE OR NOT?

When it comes to setting a realistic budget, consider whether you can afford that splurge purchase on your list. You may want to pull the room together first and then splurge on the designer pendant light, for instance. If you purchase that piece first, you may exhaust your budget with the room left unfinished. When it comes to a big money purchase, consider it but don't count on it. If the rest of the room is finished and you can still afford that statement piece, go for it – buy the pendant and rock it! If you don't have the cash, consider it as a potential future purchase to save up for, and find a creative solution in the meantime. Who knows, your creative solution may grow on you and you may forget all about the designer light!

indie craft markets online and off, or in speciality stores that sell handmade items. Everything that is made well and by hand should cost more than mass-produced products, so it's important not to compare prices for handmade items with goods that are made in factories. There is no comparison. An individual maker, conceiving and creating something in their atelier, is offering one-of-a-kind items that need to sell at a higher price in order to earn a reasonable profit. It's good to keep this in mind.

Inexpensive things can be good too. In fact, there are some stores known for carrying inexpensive quality items – Japanese retailer Muji comes to mind. Before making a purchase, consider how long you plan to keep it and how often you will use it. If you plan to use something daily, that should affect the quality and/or beauty of the purchase. I wouldn't want to use a bath towel that feels like cardboard each day yet invest in a silk pillow on my guest bed that I see only once in a while.

Draft a list of the things you use each day. When it comes to supposedly everyday items such as cutlery, hand soap, bath mats, bed linens and so on, think about what really matters and how their qualty could directly affect the quality of your life.

Setting *your* Budget

It's time to create a budget that works! Push yourself to find smart solutions, ask for help and take a positive approach. Ask yourself the following questions and use the space opposite to make notes and let's tackle this head-on!

→ WHAT DO YOU NEED TO BUY? Decide what you can afford first (the total budget for the room) and prioritize from there, listing the most important thing that you need first and ending with the least important piece. A new sofa, say, should be no. 1 on your list. It's a prominent piece and will be used so frequently that buying quality is key, so you can expect to spend most of your budget on it. If you've allocated more to your curtains, say, I would suggest reconsidering your approach – a good sofa will trump great curtains every time.

→ DO YOU PAY A PREMIUM FOR QUALITY? When it comes to furniture that you use often, always look for quality. While it doesn't have to be a designer piece or expensive, you will always either pay a bit more for something made well or need to invest a good amount of time researching quality options to fit your budget. So you are going to invest either money or time in a good piece (usually both), but once the important purchases have been made you can easily redecorate in the future without having to factor in a new sofa, for instance. You can put your money into something that isn't a must, like gorgeous curtains or bespoke wallpaper.

→ IS YOUR BUDGET REALLY RESTRICTED? Factor in what you must have first, such as curtains for privacy, a cabinet for your television, refinishing your hardwood floors. If there is money left over,

you can work in the extras that you want, but don't necessarily need immediately – wallpaper, an extra chair, an area rug.

→ DO YOU NEED TO DECORATE MORE THAN ONE ROOM? Consider decorating only the rooms that you use frequently first. If you want to redecorate your entire home, or if you are moving into a new space and starting from scratch, consider first pulling together your kitchen, bathroom, bedroom and living room. From there, you can take on the spare bedroom, dining room and sewing room. Determine which of those rooms can wait until you have time to save up.

→ HOW DO YOU KEEP TRACK? Create a separate budget for every room. You'll want to list everything that you need, again starting with the most important. A list in a notebook or, better yet, a dedicated spreadsheet is the way to go for recording all expenses. Track the estimated expense and the actual expense. This will help you to see how on track you are (or not) and where you need to make adjustments.

→ WHAT DO YOU HAVE TO WORK WITH? What you dream of owning may not be what you will end up with. For instance, I want a completely new bathroom but I know that this isn't something I'll be seeing for a while. If you rent your space, as I do, you may not have much control over certain things like your tile, flooring or kitchen cabinetry. Consider your overall approach by assessing what you have to work with, both the positive elements and the negative. Instead of weighing yourself down with what you cannot change, think about what you can change or come up with a creative solution to deal with it. For instance, you may not be able to install a built-in linen cabinet, but you can find a freestanding cabinet at a flea market to clean up and use – this is a good solution. Consider creative ways to enhance the space, which is especially important if you have a tight budget.

My budget

Think about what you would like, and what you have to spend. Allocate a figure for each section, then enter your total to see where, if necessary, you will need to make savings.

It's all about getting creative and often a tight budget can force you to use your imagination, which can lead to a space that is both unique and filled with personality and flair.

- Contractor costs

- Flooring

- Paint and wallpaper

- Soft furnishings and fabric

- Pieces of furniture

Total spend:

How will you use the room?

Knowing how you'll use a room will make a huge difference as you begin to plan your new room scheme. Many homes combine spaces to maximize square footage – living rooms with dining areas, kitchens with living rooms, offices with bedrooms, etc. It's best to decide early on how you envision it by considering if combining can work for you.

When considering a bedroom, you'll need to think about those who sleep there and how much space and storage they require. Do you like to work and watch television in your bedroom or do you keep it solely for sleeping? For young children, the focus should be on making the bedroom design as transitional as possible, with play tables that will turn into desks, toddler beds that will adapt as the child grows. Think about storage also – you know you can never have enough.

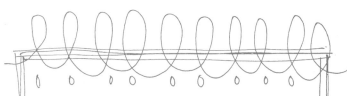

YOUR LIVING ROOM

Will you entertain there frequently? Will children play in this space? Do you need room for A/V equipment? If so, what do you need to store (DVD player, TV, cable box, gaming system, sound equipment)? When the family gathers, how many seats are needed to comfortably accommodate everyone? Do you exercise there? Do you need to create a workspace? A reading corner? Do you need to include a table and chairs for eating?

. . .

YOUR BEDROOM

Will you work there? If so, you may want a pretty desk with a comfortable chair. Are you soon to have a baby? You may need to set aside space for a crib. Do you want to read and relax? A corner chair may be nice with a reading light. How about yoga? Keeping some floor space free or creating a special nook intended for exercise and meditation might work for you.

FAR LEFT: In a small room meant for sharing, this nursery for twins works because each bed is placed along a wall with a shared table in the middle and overhead shelving as a focal point against a grey wall.

LEFT: Consider your storage when you are deciding how to use a room because most rooms require some, if not a lot of, storage. In this bedroom, it was impossible to add a door to the wardrobe because it could not open and close next to the nearby wall. A folding door was not an option as the space was too narrow, so a subtle curtain and rod were installed to blend in with the wall colour thus concealing the hanging space, making the bedroom free of visual clutter.

OPPOSITE: In large rooms you can contain more than one function. You may dine in your living space, for example, so you'll need to set aside room for each activity and think about the furniture you'll need. In this glamorous room the elegant glass dining table echoes the coffee table in the adjacent sitting area.

'This living room doubles as a sleeping space. A chaise-as-sofa is concealed by day with cushions propped along the wall to give the appearance of seating. The beauty of planning ahead and knowing what you want your room to do for you is that you really can have it all – you don't need to knock down walls or move into a new home. Get creative and make your space fit your lifestyle.'

What do you enjoy doing in these rooms?

- In my living room . . .

- In the kitchen . . .

- In the bathroom . . .

- In my dining room . . .

- In the home office . . .

- In the bedroom . . .

- In the playroom . . .

- Where the kids sleep . . .

- Other rooms in my home . . .

STEP 4 PREP YOUR SPACE

' Preparing your space may sound a bit ho-hum, but now that you've identified your project it's time to jump in and get this party started. Taking a good look at what's already there will help you to move forwards to re-create the space as you want it. '

In many ways, decorating is a lot like cooking. First, you figure out what you want to cook and then clear a workspace and clean the surface, select the right tools for the job, pull out the needed ingredients, clean and prep the food, weigh and measure everything and begin the process of whipping up something wonderful, allowing yourself the freedom to improvise along the way. In a similar way, you'll need to prep your room for what is to come as you move forwards on your decorating project. Now is the time to sort through your stuff, clear the clutter, take inventory and measurements of what you have, clean the room and begin listing what should stay, what should go, what's on your wish list. You can then remove what isn't working so that you have a clean slate to build upon. Ready to get started?

So what have *you got?*

Whether your space needs a little tweaking or a major overhaul, knowing exactly what you have to work with and having a list of measurements paves the way to a smoother journey. I spent 12 years managing and planning space for major companies and then for private clients, so I know how critical this part of the process is – and how you can run into some huge planning issues if you neglect doing them. Here are some space-planning ideas that should make the planning stage much easier.

I'm a list lover! If I don't make them I get very little accomplished. Ticking off each 'To Do' gives me a tremendous sense of accomplishment and fuels me to push ahead. While lists aid in focus and can be very helpful, they can also lead to a total state of inactivity or worse, a panic

MEASURE

You'll need to take some measurements once you know what will stay in the room and what will go. Make sure that you keep your numbers on you at all times when you are out and about shopping. Here is a list of some measurements that you will need to gather before you venture onwards. Measure . . .

• • •

The entire room, wall to wall and floor to ceiling

• • •

Your doorways (height x width)

• • •

All windows

• • •

What you intend to keep in the space – large pieces of furniture, for example

• • •

What you intend to buy – record these as you research your options

attack if they are too long or filled with goals that are far from realistic. To avoid burning out before I begin, I keep my decorating lists short and sweet. The most important is the Wish List. This is where I list all of the items for the room that I would love to buy, things I can afford and things that are incredibly over the top. The next list is my Reality List. This is where things that I can imagine realistically affording (or saving up for) are noted.

The final list is called Creative Solutions. Many decorators refer to this as the Happy Medium or Compromise List, where you outline what to settle for if your budget doesn't run as far as you would ideally like. But I prefer coming up with a creative solution over simply settling. I don't feel motivated if I think I'm settling, whereas if I view something as a creative solution I work even harder to make that creative solution a really good one that I can be proud of. Homes that are decorated the best, in my opinion, are ones loaded with creative solutions that seem intentional and not merely a compromise or 'filler' idea until the better option can be executed.

After identifying what you love, consider how you can better spotlight it. A beautiful pendant light could shift the focus to your gorgeous ceiling, and removing large area rugs and replacing them with smaller ones would reveal more of your lovely floor.

Where is your heating vent? Radiator? Air conditioner? It's important to factor these into your floor plan up front because you don't want to block them.

How will you use the room? Is it large enough to create a few different zones, for instance a living/dining combo? Bedroom and home office? A space to watch TV and cosy corner to read? How can you disguise the things you don't like in case you cannot remove them (boxy television, low ceilings, flooring you cannot replace)?

Consider the flow of your space – where people enter and leave, additional doorways that may pass through to other rooms or an exterior space such as a patio or balcony, and how people will move around within the space. You want your sofa to be a comfortable distance from the coffee table so that knees aren't knocking against it. And you don't want the table floating somewhere in the centre of the room unreachable by anyone once seated.

Consider your doorways and which way a door swings as that can affect furniture placement. Also consider what you can fit through your door – this could create a delivery problem if your sofa is too large to fit into your apartment so measure the doorway to your room and to your home in general, including the hallway and front door.

In addition to noticing in which direction doors open, think about how your windows open (in or out, tilt or sliding) and if there will be ample room to fully open cupboards, china cabinet doors and dresser drawers. You need to be able to open all furniture doors so you can access what's behind them and when it comes to drawers, you have to open them fully for best use.

How do I get it *on paper?*

You've considered some key points so let's get to work and map out your space! I like to begin with a simple sketch using graph paper and a pencil and I do not bother drawing it to scale – not yet. This is a way for me to look at my space quickly and to envision a few alternatives without making a commitment.

I've been drawing floor plans since I was child because I loved moving around our furniture – my obsession with decorating began when I was around eight years' old. Professionally, I've been drafting floor plans for over 15 years. For those of you who haven't spent most of your lifetime obsessing over the best place for your furniture, this may be a bit challenging but you'll get there, have faith! Sketch something rough first and draw up a few scenarios as to how you can imagine the space.

→ TAKE AN OVERHEAD VIEW The way I begin to sketch out the room is to view it from above, so the shape of the room will most likely look like a square, L-shape or rectangle. I grab a pencil (more forgiving than a pen) and sketch chunky lines showing where the windows are, the radiators, fireplace, doorways and anything else fixed that I am not planning to change. Next, I imagine where I'd like my furniture and area rugs. Try to create up to five different versions – one of them will work brilliantly.

→ DRAWING TO SCALE You can try 3D software or sketch it out on grid paper using a ruler, and even go as far as creating life-size paper templates of your furniture. However you choose to do it, the best idea is to create one drawn to scale for the sake of accuracy.

→ TRY OUT YOUR IDEAS Don't let this exercise cause you anxiety – in reality there are many different floor plans that will work in a single space so try a few different ones and see what ends up feeling right. Intuition can guide you, along with your tape measure, pencil and a sheet of grid paper so don't get so caught up in the numbers that you forget to tap into your creative toolbox along the way!

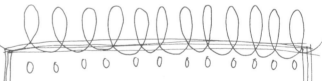

DO FLOOR PLANS SCARE YOU?

If you lack time to draw a floor plan to scale or if this step is holding back your progress because you simply hate working with numbers, hire a decorator, architect or designer to work on your floor plan for you. Specify early in the conversation that you only need to hire them for space-planning assistance and that you will do the rest. If you don't know where to start, there are several e-decorating services with savvy designers who can help you online that can be both cost-effective and convenient. A simple search online will lead you to them if you search under 'e-decorating' and 'online decorating services'.

DIFFERENT WAYS WITH SPACE

- Consider creating a few different spaces within a single room and make note of these tricks on your floor plan so you can incorporate one of these clever ideas into the final room scheme.

- Think about clever flooring, such as rugs. A rug acts as a divider, or frame, if used properly. For instance, a rug beneath your seating and sofa table defines that space as your social/TV area. A second rug in the same room beneath a dining room table and chairs defines that as your eating and entertaining area.

- Try using furniture. Float a desk in the room versus against the wall, float a sofa in the room with a console table behind it, use a room divider screen or panel to separate space or a bookcase with open see-through shelving.

- Have you thought to divide a room using a ladder? Leaning one against the wall can create a visual break between two spaces and can be a lovely spot for displaying favourite textiles.

- Wallpaper or paint work, too. Use it only on part of a room – for instance, in the area around your night tables and bed to define the sleeping space, or around your sofa to define the living room. You don't have to wallpaper or paint the entire room, only particular areas that you wish to separate from others. This works really well in larger rooms, too, especially a loft or similarly open-plan home.

- If you have the space to play with, consider introducing either a permanent or temporary floating wall. In a bedroom, if your headboard is against the floating wall, you can conceal a walk-in wardrobe or simply place the bed in a different place if your current room only has one position for the bed. Since the wall is floating,

it can also be relatively easy to mount a sound system into it, hiding the stereo in the back.

- Fabric is a great way to define a space, especially in a more open-floor plan. If you want a living room and an office in the same room, float your sofa in the living room and drop a sheer fabric panel behind it, placing your desk behind the panel to keep it separate. You can also drop fabric on a wall, too, for definition. Sew a pocket along the top edge and hang it as you would a curtain along a slim pole, or wrapped casually over a branch or large piece of bamboo for a more natural look.

HOW I PLANNED
MY SPACE

Eero Saarinen's pedestal table was a must for my creative corner. I love relaxing near a natural light source to craft and write. I find a round table visually appealing because the curves soften the lines of the room. It's also practical because there is room to move around and the cabinet doors can be opened with ease.

This room is more than just a pretty table and some chairs, it's the heart of my home! This is where I work, teach, have consultations, enjoy dinner and entertain friends and family. For this reason, I carefully selected a table large enough to accommodate my needs.

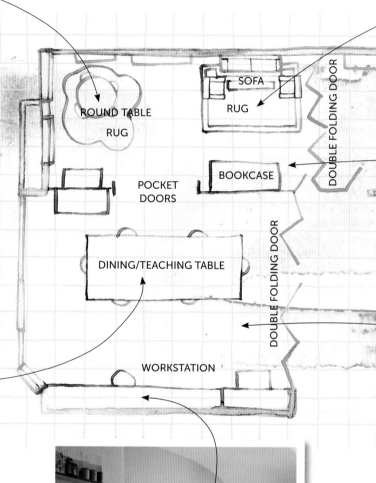

This nook was the perfect place to to install a workstation because it is recessed and also there is a small window to allow sunlight and fresh air. I customized the desk so it fits perfectly and provides me with plenty of space for assembling, printing and storage.

ROUND TABLE
RUG

SOFA
RUG

DOUBLE FOLDING DOOR

BOOKCASE

POCKET DOORS

DOUBLE FOLDING DOOR

DINING/TEACHING TABLE

WORKSTATION

I added a small seating area here for my students to mix and mingle. When consulting with clients, we frequently have coffee here and more informal discussions. I also love this corner to enjoy only with my friends and even alone while reading a good book.

SOFA

RUG

TV CABINET

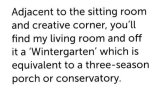

Adjacent to the sitting room and creative corner, you'll find my living room and off it a 'Wintergarten' which is equivalent to a three-season porch or conservatory.

ENTRANCE HALL

Here is another view of my studio space – this is what you would see if you were seated at my pedestal table. These two rooms are separated by pocket doors. I spend many hours at this table with clients and students and absolutely love working here.

From this perspective, you can see into my living room from the sitting area. The rooms are separated by two sets of folding wooden and glass doors from 1900 that are original to this apartment. In the summer, I love opening all of the doors and windows to create a loft-like feel.

DEALING WITH A LARGE SPACE

Do you have a huge space to call your own? Well, congratulations
– lucky you! But having acres of emptiness can feel intimidating.
Zoning is the way forward. Work out exactly what you need to do
in your home and start plotting where each of these activities is
to take place. Take note of where your services are – the obvious
point to position your kitchen unless you want extra expense and
disruption – then consider daylight, proximity to windows and the
route of human traffic through the space on a daily basis. On this
and the following pages you can see two great multi-zone homes.

' When planning a multi-functional space, it's important to create well-defined zones, not only for aesthetic purposes but for the overall flow of the space. '

OPPOSITE AND ABOVE: This is a great example of an open floor plan. The home of photographer Emma Lee, in East Sussex, combines the living room, dining area and kitchen into a single multi-functional space in the main area by creating different zones that allow her a great deal of flexibility.

Since this home is not her primary residence, she has to keep it a bit minimal, which I like for a second home – less is more when you have a second property because it is easier to maintain. For Emma, who frequently hosts family and guests, a room with different zones gives her freedom when entertaining.

There was this sense of calm that washed over me the moment I saw this home, but even more when I walked in. This is the room that I saw first and it was love at first sight. I still remember how excited I felt to be there and to be able to work in such an inspiring space for the day.

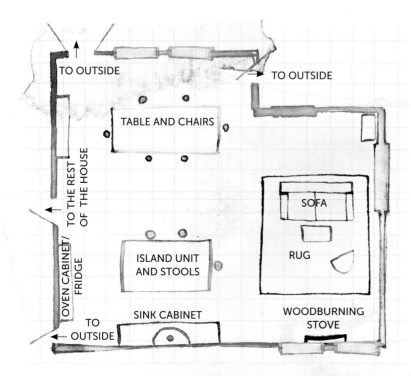

ABOVE AND ABOVE LEFT:
In the preceding pages you saw the living area of Emma Lee's modern-day drawing room, but there is more. Here you can see the rest of the space, both the dining area and the kitchen. The floor plan will help you to make sense of it all, but notice how the different zones were created by basically building everything around a central starting point. For the kitchen that point is the island unit and stools. In the dining room, the zone is established through the lighting and table. (Note: please check out the white paint on the bottom of those stool legs, definitely something to try at home if you like the idea!) The living room has the large natural handwoven jute rug as its centre, and the zone is grouped around that.

Floor plan labels:
TO OUTSIDE
TO OUTSIDE
TABLE AND CHAIRS
TO THE REST OF THE HOUSE
OVEN CABINET / FRIDGE
ISLAND UNIT AND STOOLS
SOFA
RUG
TO OUTSIDE
SINK CABINET
WOODBURNING STOVE

THIS PAGE: The dining area is in the perfect spot with the table positioned near double doors that open to a large deck with forest views. By placing the table near to doors and windows, natural light is maximized and it is a breeze to serve food that has been prepared on the barbecue in the warmer months. In a large space like this one you have to make choices in advance as to where to place each zone, so always consider how you want to use each section and then consider what needs to be available to you and your guests.

' Isn't this a most uncommon and stunning space? It is a great example of another well-planned open space, this time in a city home. '

OPPOSITE AND ABOVE:
Located in Paris' 10th arrondissement, near to the Porte Saint-Denis, this historical loft space is part of a triplex that dates back to the late 1800s. It is shared by Laure Caumont and her husband Bertrand, the team behind Maison Caumont, along with their three children. The main floor is composed of an open space with a hallway that has a custom-made glass and metal partition, two areas for seating, a cloakroom, dining space with a built-in cabinet and a large working kitchen with a pantry – you can see more of it on the following pages.

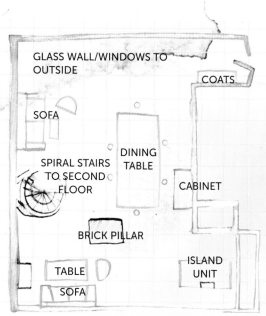

' This space works because flexibility is a key feature – everything can move around (with the exception of the kitchen), making it great for a large family and for parents who love to entertain. '

ABOVE: The iron spiral staircase makes such a statement, don't you think? It leads both to the lower level and the top floor of this home. The exposed beams, cast iron columns, brick walls and soaring ceilings called to me when I was scouting for property to include in this book – I found this home to be so authentic, warm and full of character, but also quite poetic and natural. The exposed brick and beams are warm and tactile, which lends a certain cosiness to the home despite its expanse (I got lost a few times when I was there!).

OPPOSITE: To make an open plan like this work, you need to consider what activities work together and what people will be doing in the space . You can then create your zones while making sure that, upon entering, it still fells like a balanced, complete space. Here the sitting area is clearly defined by the seating arrangement and the lovely painting by artist Zgarra. The scale of this painting really works well with the proportions of the room. I added the quirky little stool in front of the sofa because I think it's fun to add a little humour to a room – that element of surprise can make a space so much sweeter.

103

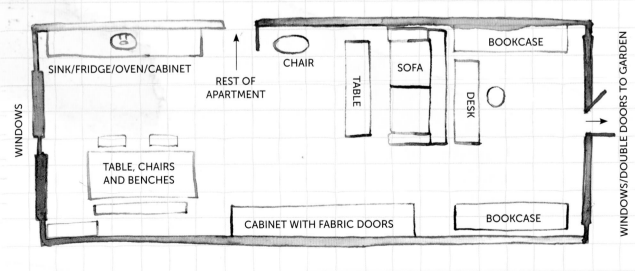

WINDOWS

SINK/FRIDGE/OVEN/CABINET

REST OF
APARTMENT

CHAIR

BOOKCASE

WINDOWS/DOUBLE DOORS TO GARDEN

TABLE

SOFA

DESK

TABLE, CHAIRS
AND BENCHES

CABINET WITH FABRIC DOORS

BOOKCASE

5 Draw up your space

A SMALLER SPACE

More restricted living quarters call for clever space management, and every inch needs to be used. In this small four-room Amsterdam apartment, homeowner and stylist Iris Rietbergen had to get creative with her space in order to make it work for her family of four. To handle all her storage she installed a large cabinet with sliding doors. In a narrow space sliding doors are a great idea as they do not hinder furniture placement – you can open them without worrying if they'll swing out and hit something. Custom-built cabinetry is another excellent way to streamline the space and to get maximum value from awkward areas.

FAR LEFT: To make the best use of the main room, Iris sectioned it into four zones: an office with built-in bookcases, a living room with storage and a television concealed in a large vintage cabinet, a dining area and a kitchen (which can be seen on pages 108-109).

CENTRE: Placing fabric on the inside of glass cabinet doors works to conceal what every busy family has but doesn't wish to always put on display – lots of stuff! This cabinet tucks away a television and other electronics, bed linens, kids' toys, Iris' stash of props, paperwork and other miscellany. It is both nice looking and hard working since it keeps the living room looking

organized and peaceful. With pattern on both the cabinet and on the facing wall, where Iris placed her favourite wallpaper, there is also a feeling of harmony – this symmetry makes the space feel balanced and welcoming.

ABOVE: This is a great way to create an office nook in a long, narrow living room space, don't you think? Take particular notice of the built-in custom floor-to-ceiling bookcase that is paired with the same bookcase on the opposite wall. This creates a sense of balance in the room, while also storing favourite book and toys.

'*Decorating follows a solid floor plan, so lay out the room first and then you can enjoy the process of prettying things up.*'

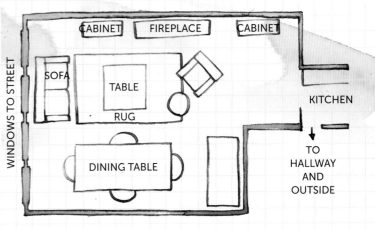

DEFINING WITH FURNITURE

A strong floor plan requires really knowing your space and how you function within it. There is not much sense in decorating without a solid foundation. Using furniture to define a space is the key to maximizing your square footage, particularly if you want to carve out a few areas within the room for different functions. Can you get more creative with your furniture layout?

LEFT: This living room in Clinton Hill, Brooklyn, was planned beautifully by its occupants, Nadia Yaron and Myriah Scruggs. They created a defined space for entertaining and relaxing by grounding the space with a rug and coffee table at the centre and arranging furniture around it, which encourages conversation. There is ample space around the furniture to move about and the chair is easy to reposition when the fireplace is in use and they face the chair towards it to enjoy the warmth.

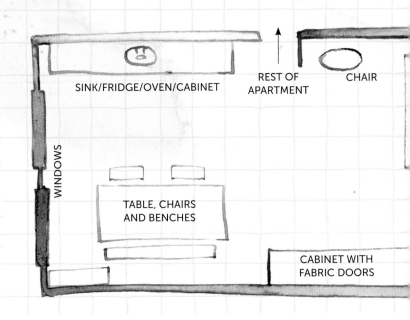

PLANNING A KITCHEN

We all love spending time in the kitchen. It really has become the hub of so many homes. So it's important to get the space right and make it work for the way you want to live in it. If you have room always try to include a table. Even a small one will give you a perch for breakfast and add valuable extra surfaces when you're cooking up a storm! For the essentials, like the sink and stove, the galley arrangement is the most flexible and can be incorporated in any layout.

SINK/FRIDGE/OVEN/CABINET

REST OF APARTMENT

CHAIR

WINDOWS

TABLE, CHAIRS AND BENCHES

CABINET WITH FABRIC DOORS

FAR LEFT: This kitchen and dining combo in Iris Rietbergen's apartment (see pages 104–105 also) really works because the layout is so functional but also smartly designed for entertaining – the galley-style kitchen lined up along a single wall allows you to effortlessly serve directly from hob to table while mingling with guests as you cook. If you have children, combining the eating area with the kitchen really works since they can do their homework or play while dinner is being prepared.

CENTRE: It is equally important when planning a kitchen that you consider your lighting and how well the space transitions from day to night. Since this kitchen and dining area is positioned near large windows, by day plenty of natural light fills the space for preparing and eating breakfast and lunch. At night a single overhead pendant illuminates the area for a more intimate experience. When entertaining, it is easy to move a large table with a bench on one side against the wall to provide more floor space for mingling while also maintaining the same number of seats. Benches are particularly put to good use in this way.

ABOVE: In some cases you may want to opt for exposed shelving to lend a more casual, open vibe to your kitchen. This shelf is only half as deep as is standard, so it doesn't overpower the sink – this makes the best use of wall space without causing the room to feel closed in. When considering what to place on open shelving, important items that are used regularly should be placed front and centre, paired with some pretty things to make the display more decorative.

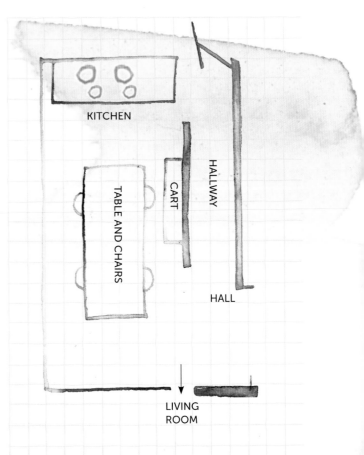

ABOVE: When it was time to renovate her space, Dutch blogger and stylist Desiree Groenendal decided to install a budget-friendly Ikea kitchen with a single line of units and a long worktop. She carefully selected appliances in brushed metal for a seamless finish and kept her cabinetry simple, with brushed metal draw pulls to blend with the appliances, giving her kitchen a professional look. Black is used quite cleverly in this kitchen in the window blinds, a single chair and a freestanding lamp since all are positioned on three different levels (low, medium and high) allowing the eye to travel around the room connecting the dots and lending a sense of space

despite the fact that the ceilings are standard height. The simple vintage table has a wooden top, which brings a tactile element to the room while the mostly white palette feels ethereal and soothing.

ABOVE RIGHT: A black rolling cart is topped with important kitchen supplies kept on display in pretty containers. Biscotti and other favourite treats are stored in glass containers and favourite coffee cups are stacked alongside containers that are used regularly. Above the cart, Desiree arranged favourite tears from magazines in a monochromatic scheme mounting them with black tape – a simple yet striking decorating idea!

KITCHEN

HALLWAY

TABLE AND CHAIRS

CART

HALL

LIVING ROOM

THIS PAGE: The kitchen is crisp, modern, bright and very Scandinavian in both look and feel. I love the layout. As a single woman, Desiree doesn't require a massive kitchen so she is able to use it as a dining space too. Desiree describes her home as a very standard Dutch apartment and it is, yet the moment I stepped in I was amazed by how she took something dubbed as 'cookie cutter' and made it truly her own.

PLANNING BEDROOMS

If you have a great bedroom, then you have a very good thing! If you don't then you can change it fairly easily so don't fret. A bedroom is where you will spend a good portion of your life, so it's best to consider it as a priority to pull together. We would all prefer to wake up feeling refreshed and ready to start the day, wouldn't we?

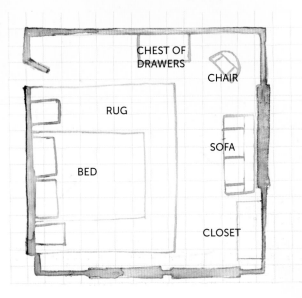

ABOVE LEFT: Add seating to your bedroom if space allows so you can read and relax, fold and place clean laundry or simply lay out your outfit. This neutral loveseat in Emma Lee's country home really warms up the space. By placing seating near a window, you can take full advantage of the natural daylight for reading. Custom-fitted wardrobes, such as this one shown, maximize the available space for storage and a nearby wicker trunk serves as both seating and additional storage space.

ABOVE: Isn't this a charming corner nook? If you place your hand over the light and chair, you may notice a big difference. How does it look with only the dresser? Not as exciting, right? The chair and floor lamp bring in their own personalities but are equally practical, and that punch of yellow really steals the show. When laying out a bedroom, try to add something in a few of the corners, like a floor lamp, chair or plant, to soften the space and make it feel less boxy.

THIS PAGE: This bedroom layout really works because the walkways are wide enough to pass through without a problem. I like that the room has a clean focus – the bed is positioned to have a view over the pretty garden upon waking up, which is better than if it had been positioned in front of a window with only a view of the opposite wall! Changing the layout of a room affects not only how the actual room looks as you enter and glance around, but also when you use it and how you interact with what is in the room and what is outside. Are you making the best use of your bedroom layout?

ABOVE: This bedroom spoke to me because of its great layout and the harmonious palette of calming tones of blue and yellow. The blue cabinet above this bed is so charming. I imagine a little one could tuck favourite books and sweet little soft toys into it. I layered multiple duvets on the bed 'Princess and the Pea' style because I find making a child's bed this way fun but also a bit quirky and different. It's a current styling trick that I like to do. Do you have your own decorating tricks that you find yourself using time and time again? It's what makes your look unique, don't you think?

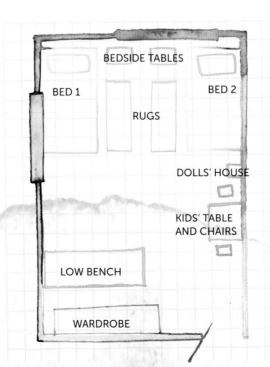

BEDSIDE TABLES

BED 1

BED 2

RUGS

DOLLS' HOUSE

KIDS' TABLE AND CHAIRS

LOW BENCH

WARDROBE

ABOVE: Crates and suitcases are a clever and budget-friendly way to furnish a child's room to add storage. They can be moved around easily when you (or your child) feel inclined to change things up. I like how each bed has its own throw rug so little feet can touch a warm, cosy surface each morning, but importantly it separates both spaces so children have a sense of independence from each other.

THIS PAGE: A shared bedroom for siblings is practical for those who lack space, and comforting for young children who enjoy the company. This particular layout works because both beds are along the wall, so there is plenty of floor space to play. When you are laying out a kids' room, consider their activities and ask them for their decorating input, too.

ABOVE: Placing furniture along the wall, rather than floating it away, works best in small spaces. I really like the metal cabinet in this creative corner. I find that most office space at home requires that you carve out a few different zones – a space to print and lay things out, a desk for your computer and a dedicated area to do something by hand, such as crafts.

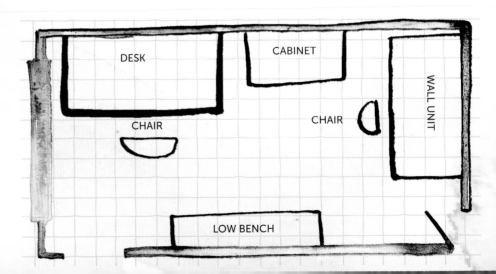

DESK

CABINET

CHAIR

CHAIR

WALL UNIT

LOW BENCH

OFFICE SPACES

An inspiring space to work at home seems to be on everyone's must-have list these days and for good reason – the right set-up can motivate and support us as well as assisting productivity. This petite office in Paris doubles as a passing through space between the hallway and the master bedroom. When working with a similar plan, consider your foot traffic and ensure that walkways are kept clear and wide enough.

CENTRE: When working on your office floor plan, consider the location of the windows so that your eyes are not affected when working on a computer and that, if it matters to you, there is a nice view to enjoy.

ABOVE: Tucking away supplies can be a problem since they are easy to forget once locked away in drawers and cabinets. Try to consider a more open approach to office organization, putting on the display the things that you either regularly use or that you regularly wish to use.

How shall I plan *my room?*

Isn't it inspiring to see how others have planned their space? Look at the ideas shown in this section to help you to kick-start the process of planning. What can you take from the various layouts and how can you apply them to your home?

As you begin to map out your space, remember that the size of your room and layout of your home overall aren't things you can change instantly, so first try to erase your dream ideas of what the perfect floor plan could be. Ground yourself in reality and try to deal with the 'what is' versus the 'what if'. Making the best out of what you have, though challenging at times, can give unbelievable results if you use a little imagination. Your room design needs to support your lifestyle and reflect your vision. You need to locate your rooms in the proper places and while some rooms are more set in stone (like a bathroom or kitchen), you may find that your dining room would be better elsewhere and that swapping the dining room with the living area could improve the overall flow of your home.

Detail how you imagine it and sketch some ideas for improvements for your home on the opposite page. When planning, try to make the most of your room's features and enhance what deserves the spotlight – a terrific fireplace surround or a beautiful garden view. Think of how you use the room and how you'd like to put it to even better

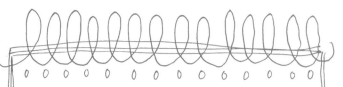

MOVING THE FURNITURE

A floor plan not only gives you something concrete to have and to hold but also encourages you to experiment with different ideas without spending a dime or getting a hernia from pushing things around. But sometimes you really do need to get physical in the space to try out different permutations for real.

• • •

If your health allows, ask for help and start moving your furniture around to see what feels right. Rearranging a space can work wonders. I've been doing it since I was a child (ask my mom!) and it never ceases to motivate and inspire me to see how quickly and easily a space can change by simply moving around a few things.

• • •

Sometimes you simply need to move that sofa of yours to a new spot and instantly your room will take on a fresh, new energy. Really. Little changes can make a big difference.

• • •

Photograph the room from different angles as you do your furniture moving, and look at the photos on your computer – it's an amazing trick that I discovered years ago and it works! Seeing your home through a photograph is eye-opening. You will instantly spot what doesn't work – trust me on this, so please try it. You always catch something you wouldn't have caught with your naked eye.

use. Perhaps you want to add a workspace to your kitchen for doing paperwork and looking up recipes on your computer? Maybe you want your office to double as a guest bedroom? List your ideas and then your alternatives while maintaining organized notes in your Project Binder. Consider what you desire in the space, too. A fireplace? A wood-burning stove? A larger sofa? More natural light?

⁶ A happy ending starts with a good beginning, so have a clean vision, confidence and a focused mind as you skilfully plan your room. ⁹

STEP 6 TRANSLATE YOUR IDEAS

' I know what it feels like to be all over the place because, as a creative person, my mind is constantly wandering off and I am an unstoppable idea generator. The only way I take control is by getting a grip. '

The more you do something, from styling vignettes to selecting paint colours, the better you will get at it over time. Remember that. These things take time and practice. Pros can immediately spot problems and find solutions because they've decorated hundreds of spaces and have literally seen it all. You have most likely not decorated beyond your own home, and I'm guessing you've not lived in hundreds of different homes to gain the experience that only decorating in different spaces can give you. Don't be hard on yourself – the more you decorate the less intimidating it will become. Even the pros have to consistently work on projects and challenge themselves to avoid stagnation. If you haven't decorated your home in a few years, it is only natural that you will feel a bit rusty but again, you can do it! Next, I'll outline how you can gather your inspirations, make sense of your ideas and turn them into something real.

ORGANIZE YOUR IDEAS

Inspiration surrounds us – we collect our favourite finds not only from books, magazines and catalogues but also from physical samples like paint and fabric swatches, feathers, a button or our favourite dress. The key is to pull all of these things together in a way that makes sense so you can edit and put them to good use, to create a room that you love!

highlight themes

It is natural to spot key themes as you gather together things that speak to you. When certain things surface again and again it can be very exciting, but also a great way to reveal a side of yourself or a particular liking that you may not have noticed before. For instance, we are all instinctively drawn to certain colours, so this is one theme to look out for as you gather. Which colours continue to emerge in all of your finds? Or perhaps it is something more subtle, such as you seem to pull a lot of rooms that feel a certain way – very relaxed and comforting, for instance, or very edgy and chic. Look for those themes and listen to what they are trying to tell you.

TIMING IS EVERYTHING

You can water down your vision if you spend too much time building out on an idea. On the other hand, if you spend too little time developing it, then your vision may not have a chance to fully develop. You can avoid wasting time and energy by simply getting started and giving yourself a reasonable amount of time to collect your ideas, collate them, edit, put everything into one place – like a moodboard – and then get started on the project. When you do that you can see your ideas turn into something very real and close to your heart.

SAVE YOURSELF MONEY

Knowing what you like and having a clear vision of what you need to make your idea a reality will ultimately help you to save money. When you're all over the place it is hard to make a sound decision, which can often result in you buying things that don't work once you bring them home.

KEEP IT TIDY

The last thing you want are storage boxes and bookshelves bursting with tear sheets. Keeping your inspirations neat and together will help you to follow through with your original vision – for instance, to redecorate the bedroom.

HAVE FUN

You can't deny how exciting it is to tap into what makes you tick. Exploring your interests is a revealing process that can help you to make important connections and decisions. Tapping in is essential as you explore your creativity and can be very liberating!

KEEP INACTIVITY & FRUSTRATION AT BAY

If you have a hard time figuring out how to decorate your bedroom it may be because you haven't started to really work on it – you are thinking about it but not going any further. Looking at the water doesn't move the boat – you have to get into the boat and row! Gathering your inspirations, determining what you want for your space and setting some concrete goals can motivate you to decorate and, most importantly, you'll enjoy the process as the journey can often be as fun as the destination, right?

BUILD YOUR CONFIDENCE

Watching your ideas take shape builds decorating confidence and is essential because without confidence it's hard to feel happy about any project we embark on. It's like working out, the more you see physical results (you can zip up your jeans without laying on the bed!) the more you want to stick with it – you feel almost unstoppable.

CHALLENGE YOURSELF

Try adding a little something wrong, something unexpected, to the mix. When pulling together ideas and translating them, examine whether or not you are falling back on what is comfortable or if you are challenging yourself in a new direction. You may constantly gravitate towards the same colour palette that you've been using for ten years but ask yourself, 'Do I really love these colours?' If you are stuck in a comfort zone then consider what you could mix in to add something fresh – a new colour or pattern, for instance. I've been adding shots of primary yellow or a dash of fluorescent pink and suddenly my rooms feel full of life.

How do I collect my ideas?

Moodboards on the wall, in books or in folders can provide a huge burst of inspiration but more than that, are known to be a smart and efficient way to build out your ideas, edit, focus and finally follow through on them.

When a great idea is left to circle in our head we often try to build it out and more ideas come, then more, until our original thought becomes so muddy that we lose track, frustration sets in and nothing becomes of those ideas – they eventually evaporate and never see the light of day. The goal is to harness your good ideas and build on them in a form that you cannot easily lose and one that you can edit within a certain space.

Are you completely overwhelmed by the idea of simply redecorating the living room, for example? We get lost on our favourite blogs, wrapped up in magazine spreads and roam stores looking for ideas, but ultimately we need direction. Many consult with professionals to help them focus on their project but I believe that is something we can train ourselves to do – a little confidence and direction goes a long way as we define our vision and map out our game plan. Moodboards, in any form, can help tremendously and are used by the pros for a reason!

Think of a moodboard as a way to visually map out how you want your room to feel and look. It also helps to see all of your inspirations pulled together in a single space, because only then can you begin to edit. I find the size of a moodboard also helps me to edit better. In my studio space I use a large pinboard for general inspiration but this serves a different purpose; it's merely to collect what has caught my eye and to inspire my everyday work (like the one shown opposite). It's motivational to me and the

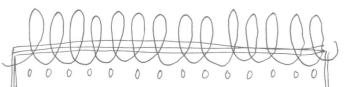

WHAT TO PUT ON A MOODBOARD

Visual reference: tears sheets from magazines, photocopied images from books, catalogue pages of furnishings, window treatments, etc.

• • •

Swatches: fabric, carpet, flooring, tile, paint, etc.

• • •

Found items: a feather, an interesting label, a piece of sea glass.

• • •

Floor plan: sketch one or use software to show how you'd like to position your furniture.

• • •

Notes: arrows pointing to specific images with notes can be helpful.

• • •

Words: add specific words to evoke how you imagine the look and feel of the room – cosy, warm, urban, etc.

• • •

If you are decorating more than one room at a time, or moving into a new home, opt for one moodboard per room. You can pull together a single moodboard for the entire home with only the colours, textures, overall style and mood represented so that you can work from that to tie the entire home design together. Work out the details (floor plans, tile work, furniture) on separate moodboards per room.

imagery makes me feel more creative and inspired. If I'm putting together a moodboard for a room they are usually much smaller – poster-board size or even smaller than that. I find the size of the board helps me to edit more critically and to not go overboard or feel overwhelmed.

' If you find a fabric that you love but cannot tear a swatch from it, colour photocopy the fabric and turn that into a swatch for your moodboard. '

today
is the tomorrow
you worried
about
yesterday

➤ MINI PORTABLE MOODBOARDS A mini moodboard can be made in a small moleskin notebook, a spiral-bound notebook or in a small photo album where you can insert your inspirational drawings, moodboards and floor plans into clear sleeves, which is helpful if you want to avoid losing snippets and to keep your collections clean and tidy. I love how portable and light these are, and that you can pull together so many things in one that can guide you on your project. I find them particularly useful when shopping. You can list all of your room and window dimensions, floor plans, swatches of paint and fabric and even current snaps of the room and swatches from soft furnishings that you already have. It's so much easier to match colours when you have them on you versus guessing as you shop, which could lead to buying a ton of fabric that doesn't match the room as you imagined it would. It's always safer to have your mini moodboard in hand!

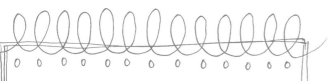

KEEP A RECORD

Take a photo of your pinboard and save the photos on your computer so that you can reference them over the months. It's a fun idea to create a new pinboard in your office once monthly. Make sure you take a photo of it before taking everything off – that way you'll forever have a record of what it looked like and it could be helpful for later. Plus it's useful to have a timeline of your personal style – the things you once liked, what you were into, it's fun!

➤ PINBOARD A pinboard (see page 125) is more of an inspirational gathering spot for everything that catches your eye – pin the candy wrapper you love, the business card with the inspiring font, tears from magazines, a postcard, a quote. This is where you collect what you love to inspire you daily. To keep inspirations fresh, try to freshen or create a new pinboard each month and build it around a single jumping off point – a catalogue tear, for example.

➤ STYLE FILES Prior to refining and editing your inspirations, while you are still hunting and gathering, start pulling things and organize them loosely into file folders. You can label them 'sofa ideas', 'living room', 'craft space', 'organizing' and 'colour palettes' to guide you. This is a better approach than stuffing everything into a single box or folder, because grouping now saves time later. If some of your inspirations easily work in multiple files – for instance, an image showing the perfect craft space also shows a great shelving system – then you can photocopy the image and use it in multiple files – for 'craft space' and 'organizing' in this example. If you have an existing collection of tear sheets with no rhyme or reason go through them and group them into folders.

➤ STYLE NOTEBOOK Tear sheets from magazines and file them according to room type in a notebook with clear sleeves. Label each of the sheets clearly, identifying exactly what you love about the room by either writing directly on the image or using a Post-it note. You may only like the chairs or the rug. It's important to home in on exactly what it is that you love about the space. I find that around 15 pages into your notebook you will begin to notice definite themes, which can be quite revealing and helpful to your project.

'A moodboard is a mood on a board, or a way of sharing visually a certain mood – how you want something to look and feel. Moodboards can help you to define your goals for a space. The more you make moodboards, the more you will train your eye and start to see your personal style emerge and blossom.'

TAKE ADVANTAGE OF ONLINE RESOURCES

- Use a social bookmarking website like Pinterest to collect your inspirations and pin those according to a theme, room, subject, etc. This is a practical way to group the things that you are responding to online and the beauty of it is that it's digital, so you can log in to your Pinterest account while you're on the road. You can create boards but you can also follow the boards of others. You can follow some of their boards or all of them, you have the option. When you click on a user's name you link to their Pinterest page where you can view all of their pinboards and explore from here. It's addictive! For a specific decorating project, create a board for that project (call it 'Living Room', for instance) and pin using the Pin It bookmarklet that you can drag into the toolbar of your browser, so that when you are surfing online and see images that you like, you simply click on the Pin It button in your browser toolbar and you can pin it to one of your Pinterest boards.

- Create digital moodboards using programmes like Picasa, Photoshop and Polyvore. Again, it's a great way to train your eye as moodboards teach you the art of editing – you can only fit so much and then you have to stop!

- Blogging can be a creative catalyst if you allow it to be. If you don't know what blogging is or how to get started then do a little online research or grab a book and you'll quickly learn the basics. I've been writing online for years. I started writing in forums and newsgroups, then on websites, and I've been maintaining a blog consistently now since January 2006. The more you record your inspirations and share them publicly, the sharper your eye becomes and your aesthetic becomes clear. The only way to make your blog truly benefit you is to only write about things that you're passionate about, not what is popular or what you think others will respond to. If you are embarking on a decorating project, and you don't already write a blog about decorating and design, consider starting a blog dedicated to your project so that you can collect and share all of your ideas there. It's also helpful if you want to share your progress with family and friends.

- Photo-sharing websites like Flickr or apps like Instagram can be very inspirational. First, they help you to become a better photographer because you will naturally grow more skilled as you take photos. Next, the social aspect of sharing your inspirations, whether it is a sign you saw on a daily walk or a flower in your garden, can also push you to keep taking photos and to keep your radar on for things that make you smile. A website like Flickr allows you to group your photos into folders in order to keep them organized, too.

→ STYLE FOLDERS If you don't have space for a huge moodboard on your wall then you can create a smaller moodboard in a manilla file folder. A file folder can be easily tucked into a cabinet and saved for future reference. It's also more portable in case you need to take it with you on a shopping trip or to share with a friend over coffee.

→ STYLE BOOKS While these take time to build, think of a style book as a very personal and (mostly) visual journal. While it's not meant to help you pinpoint a room scheme, it can become part of a valuable exploratory process to reveal what's on your radar and to grab those more abstract ideas and form them into something a bit more concrete.

I began working on style books when I was a child but didn't refer to them as that – they were just notebooks that I filled with everything I loved from stickers to teen idols, my own drawings, letters, cards, labels and anything else that caught my young eye. I find it fascinating to look back on the books that I've made to see what I was into during that time of my life.

Style books can be created using a journal with blank pages and can be based around a theme, like Country Living or Bohemian Modern. Or they can be unstructured, a space to loosely collect what you like. It can be images, swatches – anything that you can lay flat to enable you to close the book (I wrap mine with a rubber band or ribbon to hold it together).

I tend to like the freestyle approach best as I think each page takes on a life of its own, turning into a playground of self-expression, which can really unlock the imagination.

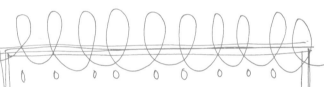

SHOP CLEVER

At a flea market, you have little time to make decisions and usually no time to drive home and measure a space to see if the great mirror that you saw will fit the space. When you have to make a quick decision, a mini portable moodboard can guide you in this way. When I have a space to fill, like a small wall or the space above a mantel for instance, I jot down the measurements in my book so that I know whether the mirror at the flea market will fit above the mantel or not. Mini portable moodboards have saved me a lot of time and frustration. As much as I love to shop I often find myself becoming quite lost in the experience of searching and lose track of what I was looking for when I first set out! My little books have saved me from burning out or coming home with a duvet when I was really in need of a few picture frames!

STEP 7

FINALIZE YOUR SCHEME

' All of the work you've done up until this point is a springboard that will now launch you forwards, opening the door of change. Allow yourself to breathe in the fresh air of something new, to smile in the face of what is to come and to feel in your heart that it was worthwhile. Bask in this moment when all of your research is about to pay off, the moment before your dream room becomes a beautiful reality. '

Congratulations, you are one step closer to the finish line! Now it's time to finalize your room scheme so that you can move on to Step 8, where you'll add finishing touches and wrap up your decorating project. It's time to narrow down all of your options so that you can pull together a final look by consolidating everything that you've accomplished up to this point. As you begin to finalize your room scheme, though, I do have one word of caution. Set a definite deadline or else you'll be tempted to research yourself into a state of total exhaustion and inactivity. I refer to this as 'analysis paralysis', which is the result of analyzing something so much that you become paralyzed by it and do nothing. That is why it's important to pull together your room scheme now and get on with it! It's time to see how your ideas pan out so you can start feathering your lovely little nest!

Create a scheme that works

While a moodboard isn't the final step before you can begin decorating (and you thought you were off the hook!) it does bring you much closer to the final stages – creating a room scheme. A moodboard plays a big part in the overall filtering process because it aids you in editing your ideas as your vision becomes tighter and more cohesive, but a definite decorating room scheme is needed.

A room scheme is the final leap between the planning of ideas and execution stage. Interior designers tend to show clients a moodboard to present their ideas and vision along with the approximate budget needed. The client then reviews their options, voices concerns, offers opinions and, once an agreement is made, the designer returns to the drawing table to pull together a definite room scheme. That final moodboard will show the client that, after all things have been considered, this will be the best approach for their project.

→ PIN DOWN THE DETAILS While it may test your patience and at times become a source of frustration to have to make so many decisions (you only wanted to decorate your dining room!) you, your budget and your room will be better for it. While you can wing it for minor redecorating projects, if you are going to totally gut or renovate a room, move into a new home, decorate a room from scratch or totally change up an existing room then it really is important to work through each and every step.

→ FOLLOW THE PROCESS You can bet that those homes that you love in your favourite magazines and books didn't just fall into place.

While some can decorate without moodboards and spreadsheets and still churn out an amazing space, most need guidance and some advice when it comes to filtering through all of their ideas and inspirations in order to make concrete decisions. I can't tell you how many people say to me that they wish they could throw things together as effortlessly as their favourite designer. But even those who protest that they've not decorated their space put some thought into it, and you can bet they are also blessed with an innate talent to put things together that gives them an edge.

→ FIND YOUR INNER DESIGNER If you didn't come into the world with interior stylist written all over your DNA, don't worry – everyone possesses creativity and imagination, it's just a matter of tapping in and developing it. Decorating is a creative exercise and though some guidelines need to be followed, the more you experiment, the better you'll become. You may eventually get to a point where you won't need to plan and prepare quite so much to pull together a room that perfectly suits you. But until you do, let's talk more about developing a room scheme.

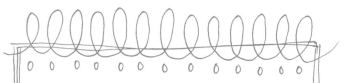

THE FINAL PLAN

Okay, so you've taken into account budget, architectural considerations, what's available to you, what you need to purchase, timing, resources, etc. Next it's time to take all of that data and create a final draft of how you intend the room to look. While you'll need to be flexible – in case the paint that you've chosen ends up not being the precise blue that you had hoped for once on the wall, for example – your room scheme is meant to take you all the way to the finish line, give or take a few tweaks.

→ GET IT DOWN ON PAPER Outline on paper exactly what you will purchase, what you will keep and what you intend to change. Also put together your final moodboard showing how the room will look, including your floor plan, final materials and the decisions you've made for paint, textiles and wallpaper. This final view will give you a chance to make any last edits before moving ahead. Now is the time to make sure that you really want that sofa or if the textile you've chosen for your Roman blinds still appeals to you. After you've spent time reviewing all of your options you can proceed.

→ MOVE FORWARDS Once your room scheme is finished, pop it into your Project Binder so you can refer to it as you go and, while you're not finished, you can relax knowing that you did it – you've reached the point in this project where you can sit back and feel confident that you made some great choices and are on your way to pulling together a space that speaks to you and makes you happy. I wish I could jump through these pages and give you a high five because I'm proud of you, you're doing great!

' *Trust me, nothing is ever effortlessly done.* '

RESEARCH YOUR OPTIONS

- Look for the best price and the most unique and appealing items, and try to get the best materials for your budget. Explore creative solutions to see just how far you can stretch your budget. Make sure you shop around on sites like eBay.

- Visit blogs, websites and e-magazines that are authored by those passionate about decorating. Get involved in decorating forums and post questions on your favourite blogs.

- Take some decorating workshops at a local art school or online and ask the teacher and students plenty of questions.

- Check out interiors magazines and other printed materials that inspire you, such as books and catalogues.

- Visit design showrooms and inspiring stores that are known to have gorgeous displays and fantastic finds or explore flea markets and large home stores where you can gather paint swatches in an array of gorgeous colours. Don't be afraid to approach sales assistants and ask tons of questions. You can do it, so start researching your options and have fun with it!

HOW I DECORATED MY HOME

I had a good time decorating this room because I was able to put my personal stamp on it and infuse it with things that I genuinely feel a connection to. I followed the steps I've given you in this book in order for my project to see the light of day and I'm so glad that I considered all of the details along the way instead of simply winging it. It feels good to walk into this room each day knowing that I created this space for myself. Happiness results from planning.

ABOVE: This is the final project scheme that allowed me to focus in on exactly what I needed to buy in order to create this room. Some of the pieces that I used include a large white wooden cabinet from Dutch firm HKliving and chairs from Tine K Home in Denmark along with throw pillows that I picked up in NYC at ABC Carpet & Home. Creating a room that works takes planning and time but once it's been pulled together you can't feel anything but pride.

OPPOSITE: The base may be white (I am limited as I'm a renter) but I layered in energetic playful colours along with some pastel tones so the room is anything but boring. I included a bright pink vintage rug to make the space come alive. This room took about 12 months to pull together since it was completely empty when I began, but the outcome was worth the time investment, as you will learn as you plan your own projects, too. Patience is key.

LIVING AREAS

Your living room is often the central meeting space where you gather friends and family, entertain and relax. Let's aim for comfort over perfection and to infuse it with loads of character and life, to create a room that you truly love that also suits the space and can evolve with now and in the years to come.

INVEST IN YOUR . . .

- **Sofa** You'll use it a lot so make sure that it's comfortable, nice looking and well made. This piece will most likely be an expensive purchase.

- **Lighting** This is such an essential part of the overall room design but also can provide the wow factor that will make it a nice focal point, too.

- **Audiovisual equipment** Most of my girl pals wish they didn't have to have flatscreen TVs and sound systems in the living room and that they usually are forced on them by their significant other. Truth be told, we all love to watch films at home and listen to music, so the happy medium is to invest in not only great A/V equipment but also in storage that conceals it or at least make sure it is well designed so that you don't mind having it out on display.

SAVE ON YOUR . . .

- **Console table, sofa table, etc.** Anything goes these days so use whatever you wish that gives you a place to rest your coffee or your feet. You could opt for ottomans with trays that you can place on top so that a single piece performs double duty.

- **Accessories** Use books, candles, a cosy throw, flea market finds, and flower arrangements to add simple decorative touches to the room without breaking the bank.

ABOVE: In the Brooklyn living room of stylist Randi Brookman Harris she has cleverly combined the best of both worlds to create a space perfectly suited to her family while also incorporating that single, beloved piece. Pairing a design classic like the organic, voluptuous Eames La Chaise with a more practical upholstered sofa marries style and comfort. While cuddling with her husband and toddler for movie night on the chaise may be a bit uncomfortable, lounging together on the sofa is perfectly cosy. Consider a similar mix of seating in your room if your goal is to blend high style with down-to-earth comfort. You can have the best of both worlds!

OPPOSITE: This chic New York apartment oozes with character, don't you think? The comfortable seating options in lush upholstery exude colour confidence and high style. When considering your seating, I encourage you to think of the size of your space first. In a smaller room, opt for a chaise and chairs without arms to maximize the overall space since these pieces carry less visual weight, which can lighten the overall look while conserving space. If you have stunning window views, take advantage of them by placing a bench below your window.

THIS PAGE: Parisian art director Jean-Christophe Aumas completely redesigned his apartment incorporating a funky yet sophisticated mix of seating with an artsy edge. Jean-Christophe was keen to imprint his love for colour and fashion on his interiors, coupled with his innate sense of style. Doors were removed to encourage flow from room to room and seating was kept minimal and light with a Scandinavian sofa found on eBay for lounging and a stunning vintage leather Swan sofa by Arne Jacobsen (1958, Fritz Hansen) along the back wall. Geometric shapes add to the playful spirit of the overall space.

Great seating

Some of the pros insist that everything in your home must be beautiful. I once concurred but I've come to see this approach to decorating as a bit impractical unless you've won the lottery! Most of us have an odd assortment of pieces collected and given to us over the years that contribute to the story of who we are and to the overall landscape of our home. I believe instead that you should simply love what you have and that everything need not be stunning. Homes with only perfectly posh pieces are highly impractical, often awkward and even a bit stuffy. Have you ever tried to relax on furniture that was extraordinarily expensive? The slightest spill or scratch could send you over the edge! When I was a child, our neighbours had plastic covers on their seating and I remember sitting on their sofa hearing a loud crunch. While we should aim to take care of what we have, I cannot live in a museum. Comfort should win over style when it comes to key pieces, though these days with the bevy of stylish and comfortable seating options available, it's easy to have the best of both worlds. Ask yourselves the following questions to decide what you need.

- Will your sofa or chair act as a focal point? If so, describe in detail how you envision it in the room and where.

- What seating do you need? A sofa – three- or two-seater – modular sofa, chair, accent chair, footstool, chaise longue?

- What activities do you perform besides simply sitting – do you lie down, work on your laptop, cuddle with your kids, eat or drink or need it to stash a bed for guests? Does it need to be stain resistant?

- When it comes to comfort, do you prefer sitting on cotton, velvet, leather, faux leather or some other fabric? Consider fillings – foam, feathers or fibre or a mix? (Foam is firm, fibre needs to be plumped daily to maintain shape and feathers are soft and luxurious.)

LIGHTING

Make sure to remember the importance of adding light to your space. It's a key player in the final room scheme so be careful not to overlook it! Consider all your options, including maximizing the natural light streaming through your windows by using tricks such as mirrors and other reflective surfaces in the room. Lighting helps you to work on everyday tasks with ease, but is also essential for creating ambience and different moods. Function isn't enough though, you also need your lighting to look good and in some cases, act as a focal point. Putting careful thought into this design element will really pay off, so shop around and light up your life!

ABOVE LEFT: Table lamps are an easy option although you do need to consider how the light falls as you do not want it shining directly into your eyes while seated in your living room. Also consider the shade that you top it with. There are various types to choose from that can alter the colour and brightness of the light in your space. This is a handmade paper shade in the home of Emma Cassi and it is not only a simple touch but it also softens and warms the lighting giving this corner a cosy feel.

ABOVE: This geometric pendant designed by the homeowner, Jean-Christophe Aumas, was inspired by Asian lanterns combined with Bauhaus and Art Deco styles. It serves as a light source while also acting as a chic focal point. Consider whether or not you want your lighting to be the shining star of the room or a supporting actor. Also consider what activities you plan to engage in while in the space, because that will influence your choices of fixtures and placement. You'll need more than one kind of light since most rooms perform multiple functions.

THIS PAGE: Floor lamps are great additions to a room and this vintage photography lamp from a Belgium flea market doesn't disappoint! Also notice the flush mounted fixture on the ceiling, chic but discreet – a good choice in a space where the floor lamp is the star. Grouping candles on the mantel lends a soft, romantic glow at night. I included the disco ball in this shot to show you a fun way to maximize both natural and artificial light. Reflective surfaces bounce around both natural light by day and artificial light by night so consider glass, metal, mirrors and high-gloss wooden floors to optimize your light.

KITCHENS AND DINING

Cooking brings out a very authentic, uncomplicated and often spontaneous and humorous side to people, don't you think? People are drawn to the kitchen because they feel secure and accepted there. When you're finalizing your kitchen plan keep in mind the kind of atmosphere you want to create.

INVEST IN YOUR . . .

- **Appliances** While some quality appliances aren't particularly expensive, consider buying the best ones that you can afford.

- **Work surfaces** You use your worktops daily, so make sure they look great and are durable.

- **Flooring** It's hard not to notice flooring in a kitchen so if you can afford to have a great floor, go for it. It's definitely something to invest in.

- **Lighting** Everyone wants to look beautiful at a dinner party. Make sure your lighting makes you and your food look attractive.

SAVE ON YOUR . . .

- **Cabinetry** Go for a budget-friendly option. There are many choices – Ikea comes to mind first.

- **Splashback** Skip tiles altogether. You could simply paint the splashback.

- **Curtains** A simple shade or café curtains work fine – privacy isn't as important as in the bedroom.

- **Shelving** Shelves that look great and work within your budget can maximize space in a kitchen.

ABOVE: In my own kitchen, a white wooden cabinet with shelving is where I display pretty tea cans, cups and cookbooks, and since they are used daily, dust isn't building up! Above my Smeg oven, I've mounted two shelves from Ikea to display favourite things along with dishware in frequent use for ergonomic efficiency. Since I rent my apartment, I am stuck with the tilework and wall colour, though I cheated and painted a little to lend a personal touch. Luckily when I moved in there was no kitchen cabinetry so I was able to customize the space - I made it my own and am happy and grateful for the things that I have in it.

OPPOSITE: Each morning I have breakfast at this 100-year-old table scored at a German flea market for a song. It's my favourite nook in my home since the natural light is always so pretty and the views of the garden bring me peace. Since my windows are bowed and I haven't had time to order custom rods, I explored the nearby forest and found flexible, sturdy twigs that I cleaned and made into rods, placing simple linen curtains on them to soften the lines in the room. The window treatment is simple yet it gave this rental space some character amidst the sea of generic tile.

MIXING AND MATCHING

There are few pure styles when it comes to decorating and in truth most looks that we achieve in our home are usually a result of mixing and matching. When it comes to merging furniture from different styles, it's a good idea to stay within a limited colour palette. In my home, most of my furniture is grey, white or natural wood because that consistency unifies all of my pieces. Selecting woods that work well together will bring harmony, too. Consider picking pieces that have similar characteristics – raised legs on the chairs and the sofa, dressers with feet versus some with and others without, for example. Such similarities can marry pieces together.

ABOVE LEFT: Many people have pieces that simply cannot be replaced due to deeply rooted connections. Do you have pieces like this? Why should you replace them, when you can simply mix and match? A home should blend our past and present because our possessions tell the story of our life and we associate positive memories with them. How do you make older pieces work with newer ones? In the SoHo loft of Brandi Becker, she successfully mixed a sturdy table with Danish mid-century chairs for a winning combination. Despite the different periods this mix works because both table and chairs are teak – the wood creates the needed harmony.

ABOVE: When mixing and matching pieces in your dining room, another successful way to blend is to look at the lines of your furniture. A great example can be seen here in the London home of Emma Cassi. This dining set-up works because both the vintage farmhouse wooden table and the painted wooden chairs in cream have the same straight lines despite not sharing the same colour. If you want to learn how to mix things up try to either match the lines of all of the furniture around your table or the colour/wood, or both.

ABOVE: Aya Yamanouchi mixed a vintage wooden table with wrought iron chairs to create a bit of a French café vibe in her Brooklyn home. This charming eating nook works because the chairs, though different, are both wrought iron and look and feel very casual and light. If you choose to mix and match your chairs then you may want to stick to the same material (wood, iron, chrome, plastic) and also consider how they are connected in other ways. For instance, these chairs both look like they could be used outdoors in a garden or café.

ABOVE RIGHT: More experienced decorators may mix in ways you cannot logically explain but somehow just work. A good example of this is the Brooklyn home of Nadia Yaron and Myriah Scruggs. This is a casual assemblage of wooden chairs with a retro metal table. How can one explain what is based purely on intuition? Decorating should ultimately be about self expression, as with any art form. How can you explain why you've painted a canvas a certain way or why your mixed media collage works? Once you've learned the basics when it comes to decorating, and have identified what you like, let instinct be your guide.

'Pick a single statement maker, such as a quirky chair or a bright pink dresser, to infuse a little drama and to spice up the space.'

How do you see your finished kitchen?

Make your notes here about how you want your kitchen to be.

BEDROOMS

When you consider how much of your life you spend in bed, it makes sense to spoil yourself a little in the bedroom by pulling together a comfortable space. Buy gorgeous sheets. Add personality through art, rugs, blankets and bedside lighting. A nurturing bedroom is the perfect escape after a long day.

INVEST IN YOUR . . .

- **Mattress** A good mattress is the most important investment you can make, so don't compromise!

- **Bedding** Beautiful bedding feels so luxurious and so it's worth collecting over time and spending a little extra pocket change on.

- **Window treatments** Privacy is important and so are light-blocking drapery linings if you happen to face an annoying street lamp!

SAVE ON YOUR . . .

- **Rug** Opt for a natural fibre rug over a synthetic one and look for one that allows you some flexibility if you decide to change the patterns on your soft furnishings.

- **Bedside tables** You can use just about anything so why not experiment with tray tables, a simple chair, a desk, crates or even stacked books with a lamp on top? Opt for a basic one from a secondhand store – add a fresh coat of paint and change the knobs for a more custom feel.

- **Full-length mirror** Every home needs a full-length mirror. If yours is in the bedroom opt for a freestanding one with a frame that you can lean against the wall as this is a bit fresher looking that ones mounted on the back of a door.

OPPOSITE: Guest bedrooms need not be boring or hotel-like. Fill them with beautiful objects, patterns and colour to make them feel cosy and happy for your friends to unwind. This guest bedroom belongs to Los Angeles designer Trina Turk and radiates pure joy. Her exceptional taste extends beyond the bright, retro textiles with a Karl Springer side table and the Widdicomb chest of drawers. Both pieces add a stylish touch, while a simple creamy white rug adds warmth underfoot without competing with the colours in the bedding.

ABOVE: Self-expression makes us happy so allow yourself to be inspired by everything around you and experiment with what you have. Why not take out some of your favourite clothes and display them on a door, room divider or wall hooks to see how they look in your bedroom. At first they may simply add a jolt of colour and pattern, but after looking at them for a few days their prints and patterns may inspire a new room scheme. Perhaps you can pull some of their colours into your bedding, rugs or window treatments and watch your bedroom blossom.

' *Think about your critical foundation pieces. The bed is most important – that will be the key piece so it needs to be well made, comfortable and topped with favourite bedding. It will most likely be the focal point so the bed is the best place to start. From there, you'll need to consider other pieces of furniture, storage, lighting, flooring, window treatments and those finishing touches that will make it all come together.* '

FAR LEFT: When decorating your bedroom consider how you will use it – what do you like to do in your bedroom? Then pull together things that will support this. Do you read in bed? Then you need space within reach for books and adequate lighting. Do you share the bed with a partner – if so then ask what they'd like to have in the room so that it better supports them, too. In this Brooklyn bedroom, a love of reading is evident. Shouldn't your bedroom be a safe haven where you can relax and reflect?

CENTRE: UK natives Andrew Corrie and Harriet Maxwell, owners of furniture and accessories shop Ochre in SoHo, own a lovely loft that they share with their children in New York. I visited their store for the first time while working on this book and fell in love with Harriet's aesthetic, which she channels into her design choices at home, making her loft the epitome of New York chic. The clean lines of the white ash four-poster bed combined with the sleek metal tables, all from Canvas, are perfectly paired. The symmetry of the tables on either side of the bed is pleasing to the eye and also provides the couple with space to stack books or place a cup of tea.

ABOVE: I always love seeing what stylist Sania Pell has done new to her home whenever I visit. On a shelf above her bed she displays an eclectic mix of small metal votive offerings still found in Catholic churches in both Mexico and Europe, along with mirrors from India and an orchid. On the wall, her favourite buttons are randomly scattered to mimic wallpaper. Her tufted grey headboard is adorned with pretty understated buttons, while her bed is layered with handmade pillows and bedding, including the patchwork throw that she made, making her bedroom a warm, cosy space inviting relaxation and sweet dreams.

CHILDREN'S ROOMS

When it comes to planning a scheme for a child's room build in flexibilty. As children grow, so their physical needs change – a six-year-old can't sleep in a crib and a teenager might baulk at the bunkbeds he once loved. It's not worth spending a fortune at any one stage. Also address the problem of 'stuff' head-on. Oftentimes children's rooms are packed with things, which makes it harder for them, and you, to tidy. Train them to feel comfortable having only things that they use and love; this will follow them into others areas of their life and will prove to be invaluable to them.

ABOVE LEFT: Wallpaper a single wall in a kid's room with his or her favourite pattern. In this girl's room, cheery Cath Kidston Chintz wallpaper is both sweet and whimsical in blue, green and red roses. It's a good idea to check in with your child from time to time that they still like the pattern as likes and dislikes change more frequently for kids than adults.

ABOVE: Painting a vintage cupboard meant for a dining room in pale green, then lining the glass doors with floral fabric, gives this piece a girly touch that it needed to work in a bedroom as storage space without looking misplaced. Beads and dresses were placed on the knobs to soften the lines, add additional pattern and colour, and make the cupboard feel more like a closet. With throw pillows on the floor and a wooden chair topped with books, the room feels very personal and sweet while keeping everything the child needs within reach.

OPPOSITE: How cute is that elephant lamp and that sweet turquoise shelving? This arrangement really shows how less is more. You do not need to pack shelving with stuff just to fill space. Display only what is useful or meaningful and hide away, or give away, the rest.

What do I need for my bed?

- **Mattress** There are a million mattress experts out there but the real expert is you. I know what works for me (coil mattress, latex foam top with a slatted bed base in exchange for a box spring) after considerable time, trial and error. Make it a goal to find the best mattress for you, too. A good night's sleep affects everything in our life – from work to our emotions, so never sacrifice a good mattress to put the money into your wallpaper or bedding. Check comfort when shopping and don't let those store sales experts talk you into something that you'll regret later on. Recline in-store on those that you like and ask if they have a return policy. Some stores allow you to try before you buy as long as you do not remove the plastic wrapping and return it within a few days.

- **Headboards** I've had many different kinds of headboards but my favourite has to be the upholstered padded variety, because I like to read in bed. Of course, you may prefer wrought iron, wood or even no headboard at all – perhaps you use a piece of fabric on the wall or have painted the shape of a headboard onto your wall. Anything goes so experiment with whatever works, but keep in mind that above all things comfort is king. If you keep banging your head against the wall (literally) or your current headboard isn't working for you, seek an alternative – life is too short to be stressed over something that you can so easily change!

- **Sheets** Good bedding makes all the difference, so replace those scratchy or pilled sheets with sheets made from natural materials such as cotton and linen. Thread counts aren't as critical as you may think; buy the best that you can afford is my rule-of-thumb.

- **Pillows** I use two Euro size pillows, two standard pillows and two boudoir pillows on my bed, but everyone is different so go with what feels right. I love my Euro pillows because I use my iPad in bed for reading at night and they are large enough to prop up against my headboard. Think of how you plan to use your pillows, too. I usually keep the more precious, decorative ones that I've ironed on a chair while I sleep so they look nice when I make the bed each morning.

- **Duvets/Blankets** I keep a quilted blanket on top of my duvet because the blanket stays wrinkle-free, since I place it to the side at night. The duvet cover is a wrinkled mess so the blanket conceals that. It's my little way of keeping the bed neat without having to iron the bedding because, seriously, who has time for that!?

- **Valances** If you like exposed legs, then don't bother with this tip but if you're like me and enjoy a valance, then you can either go custom or buy them pre-made from most department stores. You can even make them yourself – they are relatively easy if you know how to sew. When deciding on a valance, make sure it sits exactly on the floor because the vacuum will always suck up the too-long valance (plus it looks unkempt) and the too-short valance is like too-short trousers on a man – it looks a bit wrong. I like a valance on a bed because I can conceal things. Though it's not very Feng Shui of me to promote this, I am short on storage space so winter linens and jackets go in zipper cloth bags beneath my bed. In a kid's room, a valance can conceal boxes of toys and seasonal clothes.

THIS PAGE: A handmade four-poster bed in recycled wood was the starting point for the entire decorative scheme in this Dutch bedroom. Its warm simplicity coupled with the bedding in calm blue tones, and the blue accent wall, reflect the style of the entire home, which is handmade, calm, warm and natural. The sheer window panel and ceramic dragonflies that seem to be flying away on the wall add softness, while the shelving gives the homeowner a chance to switch her displays on a whim. Layered bedding in mismatched checks, polka dots and florals resonates well in this restful space.

THIS PAGE: To add some pattern to my creative corner, I tacked up a sheet of my favourite wallpaper between my two windows – its called Harlequin, in mint green and white, and comes from Ferm Living. I placed my table near the windows so I can tap into the natural daylight that floods this space throughout the day. This is particularly important since light affects my mood tremendously and serves as a terrific source of motivation and energy. If light affects you similarly, try working near a window if you can – it can really impact your mood and even your work!

' Do you have a creative corner in your home? If not, what is holding you back? Do you want one? If you have one, does it inspire you? How can you make it better so that you feel encouraged to use it regularly? '

CREATIVE CORNERS

There are several elements that you will need to set up a creative space that works. First, identify the location and then the type of work surface and storage that you require – it's vital to assess your needs and take inventory. You might require additional work surfaces for different tasks (painting, computer, printing) so take into consideration your work style. Another important element is your chair – it needs to be comfortable – and don't forget to give yourself a bit of wall space to gather inspirations in a place where you can see them daily. The final element is to ensure you have the best lighting so you can see what you're doing!

OPPOSITE: In my sitting room, I carved out a space in the corner for being creative. The white wooden cabinet from HKliving in Amsterdam is my storage space and the Alex drawers from Ikea hold papers, scissors, rubber stamps and stamp pads – all items that I use when making things by hand. The pinboard, a sheet of cork that I covered using old linen, was mounted to the wall and is used for pinning favourite things. Mismatched chairs that sit around the table serve as extra seating for when I use this space to craft with friends or with my students.

ABOVE: This is the very pink and lovely creative space belonging to my friend, Dutch blogger Yvonne Eijkenduijn. Isn't this an inspiring setting to tap into your dreams, ideas and inspirations? Her bookshelves are from Ikea; she cleverly designed shelving to fit the entire length of her workspace, which doubles as a dining area, and topped it with a sheet of custom-made wood to marry the individual pieces. In her vintage cabinet, which she has painted white, Yvonne stores a few of her favourite things, from yarn to stationery, which double as display.

Carve out a space to create

Most of us have a favourite place to hang out at home, our own little sanctuary for enjoying a cup of tea while flipping through a magazine. Think about it for a moment, do you? If so, where is your one spot that you seek out for reading, working, reflecting, crafting, playing with your children? That single space, your inspiring nook, can allow you to unleash your creativity and set ideas into motion.

A cosy nook can also lead to a greater sense of well-being, because it simply feels good to take time out for yourself, doesn't it? Whether you live in a large home or a tiny apartment, consider allocating yourself that special corner or a room if you don't already have one. Finding the space can be a problem for so many when deciding on exactly where their nook should be – in fact, securing a creative corner often requires creativity!

I work from home so I needed a creative corner for a desk, because my home office on the sofa wasn't working out. I decided to lay claim to an area in our rarely used dining room and it has become the perfect workspace.

TRY IT FIRST

Before setting things up, bring a chair into the spot you've designated, sit on it and stay for awhile! See if you really like being in the area. Turn the chair to face different directions – face the window, the door, the wall … What feels most natural?

A WORKING SCHEME

- **If you don't have a door** a curtain may help to visually separate the space and allow you to close it off when not in use.

- **If you don't have a whole room** you can commandeer, look for an unused space in your home – the hallway, beneath the staircase, in a corner of the living room, etc.

- **If you want it to feel relaxing** pick colours that calm you down like blues, neutrals and violet. Decorate with objects that aren't super stimulating. Keep it simple.

- **If you want it to feel cosy** add texture through plants, window treatments, throw rugs, a cushion for your chair.

- **If you want to stimulate thought** work with colours and patterns that give you energy like red, yellow, pure white, green, or a graphic combination like black and white.

- **If you want it to feel personal** bring in things that you really love, objects that make you happy. If you plan to use them for your projects and hobbies, think of creative display ideas, too – often ribbons stashed away in drawers would look so much prettier if displayed in a ribbon holder or from tacks on your moodboard.

- **If the space is a bit odd** – tiny, extremely narrow, an odd-shaped alcove or perhaps a hidden niche – then consider customizing it with built-ins. Floor-to-ceiling bookshelves, storage cabinets, a window seat, a custom workspace – the investment is often worth it because you can fully utilize every square inch. If hiring a cabinetmaker isn't in your budget, opt for a more do-it-yourself version and get imaginative at your local Ikea.

THIS PAGE: If you're not a fan of pinboards, opt for floating picture ledges, such as these ones from Ikea, placed above your desk. They are perfect for rotating objects that catch your eye and allow you to freely place your inspirations as they hit you.

What do I need to do when?

Pulling together a precise 'To Do' list, or a Decorating Schedule, is essential because it can save you time, money and some headaches (not all), and you'll definitely have an advantage over those who opt to wing it, only to realize they'd forgotten to call the painter and now he's booked solid for the next several months, which delays the project (and no one wants that).

You can list everything on paper with columns and check them off as you go (my preference) or you can use a spreadsheet if that works better for you. At the most basic level, your schedule could look like the

KNOW WHERE TO FIND IT

When your decorating schedule is pulled together, keep it stored in your Project Binder and update it as you go, returning it to the binder for safekeeping. If you've decided to maintain a spreadsheet on your computer then keep it in a folder named after your project so that it will be easy to find. I keep active projects on my desktop in a file folder for quick reference and in them I store everything from spreadsheets to notes, images, invoices and anything project-related that I need to keep together.

sample below: use the blank one for your details. Or you could add in costs, notes, contact information, etc. If you prefer that approach, use the space opposite to start plotting your targets.

TASK	SUPPLIER	OTHER DEPENDENCY	COMPLETED
Decide on exact tiles	Fired Earth	None	28 March
Purchase tiles	Fired Earth	Decide on what I want first	28 March
Call tile guy to set install appointment	Tony the Tile Man	When tiles arrive	5 April
Tile installed	Tony the Tile Man	Tile delivery	10 April
Order shower curtain	Anthropologie	Tile selection	29 March
Buy brushed metal (silver) curtain rod	John Lewis	None	29 March
Install shower curtain rod	Tile guy can do this	Purchase rod + install tiles	12 April
Buy rings for curtain	John Lewis	None	29 March

TASK	SUPPLIER	OTHER DEPENDENCY	COMPLETED

Write your schedule here

STEP 8 HAPPY DECORATING

' Now you can move beyond the practical elements. The ultimate goal when it comes to decorating your home is to put yourself into your home, meaning you have to personalize it, work your magic, stamp it with your individuality, make it eclectic and deeply personal and allow it to reflect your life. There is nothing quite like finishing touches, the icing on the cake, the cherry on top! '

Now you can allow your creativity to shine and decide just how much impact you want your room to make. Are you going for a subtle homespun vibe? Pay attention to details like delicate trim-work on curtains, handmade blankets and embroidered napkins. Do you want to make a bold statement with pattern? Play with scale, mix in some bold fabrics, paper a wall. Adding personal touches comes more naturally once you have homed in on the vibe you're looking to create, placed fear aside and made the decision to dive right in! Decorative cushions, handmade elements, cosy rugs, a stack of gorgeous blankets on top of a cabinet . . . All of these personal layers give a room dimension and soul, which is why I love the little details so much.

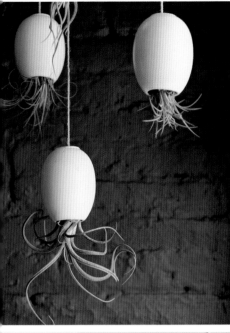

THE POWER OF PATTERN

One of the ways to give any room an individual touch and decorating lift is with pattern. Pattern can wake up a space and elevate it to a whole new level, so it's a good idea to put some thought into what you are trying to communicate.

Do you want to have a Scandinavian vibe? Opt for bold graphic prints such as geometric prints, over-scaled blooms, stripes and dots. Perhaps you have a sweet country look in mind? Brightly coloured florals paired with stripes may do the trick. Look at your favourite rooms in magazines and note what patterns you are responding to. Tear them out and see if you can source them and order swatches if you can. I have an entire cabinet filled with fabric that I refer to constantly. If you can't find anything in magazines that you're responding to, take a peek inside of your wardrobe. If you don't tend to wear a lot of pattern, investigate your accessories instead – the lining of your favourite purse or wallet, a scarf, socks and even your lingerie drawer may reveal the patterns that you love that you never gave second thought to until now. Next time you're shopping, take some snapshots of patterns that give you a positive emotional response. It could be in a store or on the street and range from street art to billboard advertisements or product packaging. When you get home, look at all of your photos together and see what recurring themes exist. Intricate patterning? Clean lines and geometrics? Organic patterns? Your pattern preferences are trying to tell you something – use them in your home!

ABOVE: A few well-considered yet simple touches can elevate a bedroom. For the ultimate of comfort, add an upholstered headboard in your favourite colour or pattern and build the space around it. In Brandi Becker's New York loft her master bedroom is calming in shades of indigo and brown. This colour combination is warming and appealing to the eye and her mix of patterns on the bed combined with the artwork adds visual interest, using both scale and tone to make this sleeping space soft and welcoming.

OPPOSITE: In this inviting Brooklyn home natural tones take centre stage yet subtle pattern is introduced in quieter ways, making this space feel like home. The handmade wooden cabinet with its sliding doors adds texture and pattern while other understated elements bring in pattern like that small striped vase, the blocks of colour on the rug, a woven seat, fireplace wood casually placed beneath the cabinet, tile work around the fireplace, the patterning on the hardwood floors – all of these fine patterns lend comfort and style. You can add pattern discreetly for a similar effect.

OPPOSITE: When James Leland Day gave me a little background on his sofa, I fell even more in love with this arrangement in his living room. Nearly abandoned on the streets of New York, James grabbed the leather sofa and brought it with him to Paris. Unloved, torn, a little worn, some of this is a welcome change in a room. Often that very element of wrongness warms up a room because it's less fussed about, which can be a good thing as naturalness is inviting. If your seating is a bit imperfect you can always add a simple throw and a few cushions, which also bring in colour and pattern.

ABOVE: After we shot James's apartment , I felt so inspired that I went home and created my interpretation of his living room using objects around my home gathered on a tabletop. I love all of the pattern, colour and texture in this arrangement. I even worked in an antique book with a golden 'L' embossed on the cover in homage to James. Trying to recreate a room scheme in a similar way is a good exercise for building confidence with colour and pattern. You can get started easily by working from a favourite image in a magazine. Give it a try and see what you come up with.

PLAYING WITH PATTERN

If you find a space you're inspired by, it can be interesting to gather a collection of items and samples that the scheme suggests, as I have done here. This creative exercise more than likely will not end up as a room in my home; however, it challenged me to look at colours and patterns that I do not typically use in my space and work with them even in a small way to expand my horizons and have a little fun.

HAS PATTERN BEEN THERE ALL ALONG?

- What patterns made you happy as a child? I have long had a love affair with pattern, which began at a very early age and through a simple yet effective creative exercise – colouring! I enjoyed creating both geometric and floral patterns with my crayons instead of using only solid colour and I rarely stayed within the lines – my patterns and doodles extended far outside of the prescribed space meant for applying them.

- This love and sheer fascination with pattern also affected my purchasing habits as a young girl, too. My favourite store was a Japanese stationery shop that I would frequent every Friday, spending my entire allowance on patterned papers, journals, pencils and stickers.

- Flea markets and home stores were another love and I would accompany my mother on her trips. Some of my favourite things included bedding, sofa cushions and shower curtains, all beautifully patterned in florals, dots, plaids and stripes, with a few animal themes thrown in because who doesn't love a few birds? My bedroom was loaded with pattern in mostly florals in all sizes, from sweeping bold blooms to tiny buds, for the ultimate feminine space.

- When you look back on your childhood, what kind of pattern did you surround yourself with? Block patterns in bold colours and shapes? Small florals? Polka dots? Stripes? Do you see any hint of this today in your grown-up interiors?

ABOVE: Pattern can be expressive of a feeling, time, place or associated with a specific period – retro patterns from the 1970s may echo those from our homes as children, bringing us a wave of nostalgia. Pattern can have strong cultural, historical, religious and political associations too. Most patterns are also very specific to time periods, allowing you to research them in order to pinpoint their origin. That is why exploring the world of pattern and then bringing it into your room through the objects that you put on display can be such a powerful addition to your room scheme. A tabletop vignette is often the easiest way to bring in pattern instantly.

OPPOSITE: A home without pattern is like living without the sense of taste. A meal may look and smell delicious but taste is what we look forward to the most when eating, in addition to satisfying our hunger cravings. If your home feels a bit uninspiring try introducing more pattern. It can be obvious or subtle, from woodgrain on a table to a bold block-printed throw from India, but work in more pattern and see what happens.

Layering pattern

I am frequently asked how to properly layer pattern because it can be both interesting and tricky, yet how you approach pattern and work with it will define your interior. So here are some easy tips that may demystify the process a bit. Ready to get creative?

- First, choose a grounding pattern as your base and work up from there. A solid colour or a subtle pattern (such as small dots) can work, for instance, as the colour of a headboard or sofa.

- Next, add in a large-scale pattern as the statement piece that you will build on. Perhaps it is a bold geometric, a floral or colourful ethnic print? I like to use it on one item in a room, on a rug, wallpaper on a single wall, artwork or bed cover, for instance. I also tend to limit myself, using only one large-scale pattern per room. It can also work on a side chair or, if you are fearless, the sofa.

- Now it's time to mix in medium-scale patterns. For some reason, I prefer my medium-scale patterns to be dotted throughout the space, in the form of slim stripes, florals, dots, etc. I also like to add in some contrasts – for instance, in a mostly neutral space with blue, I'd add in a little pure red or orange. Medium-scale patterns work on a sofa throw or as wallpaper. The key is that these patterns need to incorporate most of the colours from the base pattern and the large-scale pattern – not all but most.

- Add smaller-scale patterns next. I tend to put them on smaller items, a trim on curtains and piping on pillows, but they also work as wallpaper for those who like subtle hints of pattern, or even as upholstery for a headboard. Smaller-scale patterns need to have at least one colour from the large-scale pattern.

- Now it's time to create some tension. A friend of mine once advised me to add a little wrongness to any creative project and that stuck. Now when I create a room scheme I scout for that single 'wrong' or 'wonky' element that essentially makes the entire room very, very right. Adding a little tension can create energy and loosen things up. You have the opportunity to do this with pattern. Perhaps you are working on a mostly pastel children's room and it feels a bit bland – mix in a little fluoro pink and watch it come to life.

- Often stylists will add black to a scheme if they sense it's becoming a bit too sweet or generic to 'edge it up' a little. Add a pattern with a little black or a darker tone of the colours you are using to create drama.

OPPOSITE: The variety of patterns in this country bedroom delights the eye. From the plates to the artwork and bedding, pattern travels throughout this space in sweet harmony, rhythmic, at ease. I love how pattern can transform. Whether you opt for patterns that are painterly or more graphic (or a fusion of both), the best advice I can lend when it comes to layering patterns into a room in both the foreground and the background is to simply make sure they harmonize and of course, speak to you.

OPPOSITE: This London home also doubles as an atelier and showroom for jewellery designer Emma Cassi. Here she applied an interesting treatment to a single wall in her showroom nook using a neutral beige base and white. Emma created her own stencil and using creamy white paint, she created loose dreamy swirls. There is something quite joyous and heartfelt about it, don't you think?

THIS PAGE: This is Emma Cassi's master bedroom where she has applied pattern to her walls once again, only in a different way, to transform her sleep space. Her bedroom is quite small and a headboard is not an option so Emma dreamed up an alternative – to use her favourite wallpaper pattern, cut it in the shape of an ornate headboard and adhere it to the wall. This is so clever and despite how subtle the pattern is, it still adds a very special touch, lending character to the space. Can you think of alternative ways to use wallpaper? On cabinet doors? Inside your wardrobe? On a lampshade?

' *Children love visual stimulation, so while I may not go this crazy with pattern in my master bedroom, this sweet nursery is a dream come true for a curious baby girl.* '

ABOVE LEFT AND OPPOSITE: In this nursery in the Netherlands, homeowner and stylist Tinta Luhrman decided to add tons of retro charm using floral patterns with shades of green and brown. By building a custom wall unit for storage, Tinta was able to design it without doors, giving her more opportunity to display her love for pattern in unique ways. She brought in vintage florals through her choice of wallpaper, textiles, books, storage boxes and her daughter's sweet little dresses.

ABOVE: When adding pattern through wallpaper, think outside of the box. You can simply add strips to parts of a room or several different patterns, as shown here above this sweet little wrought iron crib. When working with pattern, consider scale and try mixing petite, mid-sized and larger prints so that some are more in the foreground and others recede so the eye can move around the room and the senses are not overwhelmed.

START SMALL

Add one or two patterned items, such as throw pillows, a lamp shade, a blanket. Experiment in a small room first – in the bathroom, say, mix and match your towels, throw rug, shower curtain and accessories.

SPOT THE BAD GUY

If something about your room scheme isn't working, gather your patterns before you, lay them all out and see if you can spot the bad guy – that single pattern that isn't playing nicely with the others – so you can remove it from the space altogether. When working with pattern, editing is critical so you end up with a combination you really like that doesn't jar.

THINK ABOUT SHAPE, SCALE AND TEXTURE

Vary your shapes – mix stripes with florals and more fluid ethnic prints, for instance. Small, medium and large are the three main sizes of scale. Try to vary scale throughout the room when working with patterns or else things can get either really blah and boring or totally cluttered. Patterns that have texture add dimension and warmth. Think of leather, mohair, embroidery, faux fur, basketweave, suede, etc.

OVERDONE IT?

If your room begins to feel a bit stressful because you've added too many patterns, don't be afraid to edit and remove some. Your bright geometric rug may work better in another room and the curtains may look better cut down in size and reworked as Roman blinds so they aren't so overpowering. Also consider neutralizing the space by introducing a large neutral accent, like a natural sisal rug or linen drapes in a pale solid colour to balance the more hectic elements you've included.

BALANCE THE TEXTURE

Notice details in patterns such as woodgrain, snakeskin, velvet and stone. A good textural mix layered into a room adds energy and interest. Aim for balance and edit texture just as you would with colour and pattern, too. You want the overall picture to feel casual and 'right' and not busy or tacky.

Soft furnishings

Upholster a chair, or your entire dining room set of chairs, in your favourite patterns. You can try the same print or a completely different pattern for each. An entire sofa is a bold move so if you're not ready opt for a side chair in a favourite print or just a single seat cushion instead.

A RUG CAN MAKE A HUGE IMPACT

Try adding pattern to your floor through a gorgeous rug and build around it. It can really define a space. Separate your living space from your dining table in an open-plan room with a patterned area rug. Area rugs should be large enough for furniture to sit on while still being able to see enough of the rug to appreciate the pattern. Rugs warm up the bedroom, giving it a cosy feel, so place small rugs alongside the bed.

WAYS WITH WALLPAPER

Patterned wallpaper can be used on walls, on a single wall, inside furniture, in doorways and on a desktop (with transparent glass to protect it). You can even wallpaper a ceiling, though if you do, either stick to walls in a solid colour (or white) or repeat the same print from the ceiling onto the walls. I steer away from introducing a different pattern here as it can be a bit bonkers!

How will you introduce pattern into your home?

If you love pattern but you're a little uncertain about how you could include it in your decoration get started with this quick exercise. Create a tabletop vignette on your coffee table using only objects found in your home to create a mini grouping of patterned objects – a plant, a piece of tile, a small painting. See how it feels to see more pattern in your space. Do you like it? Pattern is easy to work with once you get the hang of it, so be daring and practise until you get it right. That's what the pros do! Think about some ways you can add pattern to your walls and jot down some notes here. Wallpaper, stencils, wall stickers, faux treatments, wainscot panelling – there are so many options so consider a few for your next decorating project. I'd love to know what you come up with!

What do I display?

It's vital that what you have in your home speaks to you, so you're not just amassing stuff but choosing things that you make an emotional connection with. This is important beyond being aesthetically pleasing – you want your things to make your heart happy.

Sure, your sofa or coffee table may be nothing more than a place to sit that is comfortable and a piece of wood to rest your cup upon, but the layers you add onto them can lift the mood and establish a relationship between you and your space. Your favourite books on the coffee table with a few decorative elements that you brought back from trips, cushions made from fabrics you've collected throughout the years, a cherished throw given to you by your grandmother – this is the good stuff.

While you may not buy a new sofa for another ten years, you likely will tire of a lamp and buy a new one, move a chair from one room to another, or put some of your table linens in a drawer pulling others out for display. This is why decorating doesn't have an end point and that is fine. While some edit only now and then, those who love expressing their creativity through decorating may find themselves editing frequently and the beauty of regular practice means that you will typically become better at it.

Life can get so serious yet tinkering around with decorative elements can be thoroughly therapeutic at times when you feel overwhelmed or stressed. Rearranging and styling your home can also be a lot of fun and pull you out of a bad mood or make a good mood even better. When I'm feeling energized and creative, I often rearrange my tabletops or paint something, like a small table. It may sound petty but who cares, I like it, and no doubt you do too, or you wouldn't have picked up this book. There is no shame in being domestic! My hobby as

a child, which was moving my parents' furniture, pictures and mirrors on a continual basis along with rearranging bookshelves, became a hobby as a teenager, then moved more towards a job in my twenties, and into my thirties became my career.

Today, I still love being creative at home through decorating. I can channel my creativity into something that gives me an immediate emotional response – and if I don't like how it looks I can easily change it and start again. Can you relate? Adding personal touches allows us to unleash our creativity and leap from tall buildings and that just feels good, doesn't it? So let go and add those quirky touches here and there; it's your space so you have the right to let loose and get personal.

RIGHT: Incorporate a selection of precious handmade pieces in your displays, like these porcelain cards from Kühn Keramik in Berlin. Your guests will stop to notice them if they're part of a thoughtful grouping on a shelf versus stashed away in a curio.

FAR RIGHT: Consider grouping objects by colour to keep them from looking too cluttered. On this bookshelf in a London bedroom, ceramics take centre stage while books, a handmade doll, vintage finds from flea markets and paintings all contribute to the pastel-toned feminine ensemble.

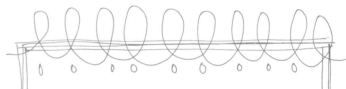

EDIT YOUR STUFF

Fashion diva Coco Chanel suggested to always remove a piece of jewellery before leaving the house, which stressed the need for editing. It's the same when decorating. Try to remove what isn't working. It's better to have just enough in your home than an overwhelming amount of stuff that seems to suffocate you. You can bury yourself under the weight of things, so edit your space just as you would clean out your wardrobe. Some have a rule in place that if they buy something they must remove another. That's a good rule! Replace what's not working, repair what is torn, add fresh pieces to update your look and mix in certain layers and textures as the seasons dictate. In the winter, you will likely mix in mittens and hats into your wardrobe. In a home, it may be leather and wool pillows and a cosy mohair throw for the sofa.

ADD YOUR PERSONAL STAMP

- It is so important to personalize your space! Just as we don't want the exact same haircut and wardrobe that our friends have, we definitely do not want to live in a home where nothing at all feels or looks like us – who we are. These days, self-expression is encouraged and freedom sought after and celebrated. This extends into dress, grooming and the way that we decorate and live at home. Decorating guidelines are helpful, decorating rules are not. Making our home look like a catalogue was widely accepted ten years ago, but then there was a shift that started to influence how we looked at design and decorating. Thank goodness!

- Decorating has evolved before my very eyes into something much bigger than most expected. Wallpaper, paint, furniture, accessories – everything has opened wide for the average consumer to see and buy with or without a designer. When I was in design school, the fact that many businesses were 'Trade Only' was a very limiting part of the decorating process that I began to dislike, as it was a frequent source of tension between a designer and client. A client often wanted designer items at affordable prices, but the market was saying that the client wasn't going to get the best of both worlds, that a beautiful home only came with a very high, exclusive price tag. If you couldn't afford to hire a designer then oh well! You could always buy generic wallpaper and furniture yourself at the local home or DIY superstore. Though trade only still exists in certain quarters, good design options finally extend outside the designer showrooms.

- Of course, that gold-star level of design definitely exists and I'm all for it if you have the bank account, but those of us who are trying to stay within a budget are perfectly happy to do the research ourselves and buy what we need online or in-store. I think we are so fortunate to have so many beautiful products available to us. That is why we simply have to take advantage of them and personalize our home. With so much on offer to tempt us, it's a good idea to investigate, to look for ways to layer in and edit out things that work and those that do not. Your home is YOUR space after all, claim it by putting your own personal stamp on it!

OBJECTS

Grouping similar objects is the trick of many a stylist and decorator. It's one of the safest ways to begin styling, so if you are an absolute beginner at arranging objects, then start by pulling together objects first. Think of what you have a lot of that are spread throughout your home. Bringing them together can make for a stronger presentation. When displaying objects, try also to tell a story, either through the colour, the pattern or the overall voice you are trying to give to your vignette. Put some thought into your arrangements so they are more artful and from the heart. Mix in pieces from your past to make your groupings more personal.

' If you have a collection of objects that you adore, such as vintage globes, typewriters or fans, opt to display them grouped together on a shelf, rather than scattered in random places all over your home. '

OPPOSITE: I love everything about this display. From the vintage maps to conceal the fireplace during the warmer months when it's unused, to the silhouette decal on the mirror, there are so many special touches and delightful objects in this photo. I like how unstructured it is, you can tell it has been done rather intuitively, and the hints of yellow and orange make me smile. What an inspiring collection of favourite things! Study the arrangement for a moment and see what you can take away for your own home. Anything you may want to try?

ABOVE: In this country home, styling books and pottery on a shelf creates a stunning display. To do something similar, collect a selection of things – books, cups, plates, for instance – lay them before you on a table and look for a theme. It could be the colour, pattern or size. Start moving things around to see which work together. Next, find a single shelf that could use some sprucing up to arrange them on. It really is that easy to start styling your space. Grouping similar objects is a great starting point though it's not just for beginners – the pros do it constantly with stunning results. The more you practise, the better your arrangements will look.

' When displaying precious things, try to lay them out nicely and put extra thought into polishing them up. Later, take time to maintain them with regular cleaning. '

ABOVE LEFT: Try showing your favourite things in the kitchen. In this London apartment, a mix of old and new hand towels add a hint of colour and pattern while the objects on the shelf were selected to be both ornamental and useful to the cook. When styling your home, consider where you need to blend both function and beauty before getting started. If your own shelving in the kitchen only stores pretty untouchables, then it's not serving its best purpose, so try mixing it up with objects you need and objects as eye candy.

ABOVE: In my cabinet of curiosities, I store favourite things collected over the years from my travels both near and far, along with my husband's cherished objects including some of the antique books that he collects. By containing our collections in a single glass curio that is French in origin we were also able to marry the antique collectibles with an old piece of furniture, creating harmony. Displaying such precious things in an Ikea cabinet would not be a good fit, so consider the relationship between the objects and where they are being placed.

' The more you act on your creative impulses and try new things, the better you get as you'll build skills and confidence. Confidence is the ultimate goal. With it you can rule the world or at least, rule your home by turning it into your own personal happy space. '

ABOVE LEFT: London-based stylist Sania Pell is incredibly gifted, particularly when it comes to producing crafty ideas for the home. I love how she created these silhouettes of flowers and vases using wallpaper, then stuck them to the back panel of a vintage cabinet on display in her daughter's bedroom. Adding dimension when arranging things on a shelf can make a big difference, so place things to the back, in the middle and then closer to the front rather than lining everything up in a single row in the middle.

ABOVE: An exposed bookcase need not be messy if you put some thought into how you organize and display your things. If your magazine spines do not complement the colours used in your room, or they are simply too busy, conceal them in magazine files. Group books with similar spine colours together. Study this bookcase and see how you could try a similar look at home.

FOCAL DISPLAYS

Do you have somewhere in your home where you could create a stopping-off point, somewhere you or your guests can pause and take time to enjoy something interesting? Perhaps you can curate an arresting collection of objects that you change on a regular basis. Or maybe you have an unusual or a striking piece of furniture that deserves a location where it can be noticed and admired. These display statements add so much to the personality of your home.

THIS PAGE: I had fun styling this display of quirky bits in the entry of this Parisian apartment. None of these objects belongs to me so I had to select what I felt worked together, but that also told the story of the homeowner based on the way that I felt while styling his space. My goal was to create something playful, uncommon and quirky – exactly like the vibe of the home. When creating a focal point be a little bold and exercise your creativity and intuition and see what you can come up with.

THIS PAGE: Furniture that makes a strong statement, such as the Lesley Sideboard designed by Fitzhugh Karol in Brooklyn, can also serve as a focal point. This sideboard incorporates various materials and handmade pulls to create a one-of-a-kind piece that you cannot help but stop and take notice of. Look for a single grand piece of furniture that you can add to the mix in your own home. My grey cabinet from France is currently my statement maker and focal point. What is yours? How can you better highlight it?

CABINETS

I love cabinets as storage, for displaying my favourite possessions and as decorative pieces of furniture in their own right that can be customized to add your own stamp. For instance, on the cabinet shown left the back panel was painted black so that the objects on display are more pronounced. I also adore that random strip of kelly green on the front – unexpected quirks can be pure magic. When using cabinets think of painting the interiors or adding magical touches of your own.

I especially like cabinets that have glass on all three sides – because their contents can be viewed from any point in the room they add real decorative value. When arranging things in a cabinet that you can see from many sides, examine your arrangement from left, right, then centre to make sure that it works from any viewing area.

' Freshen your display cabinets regularly by removing everything, then edit what you wish to show and avoid overcrowding. '

OPPOSITE: This vintage medicine cabinet, repurposed in the kitchen to store and display assorted ceramics, pots, glasses and bowls, is the first thing that you see when you walk into this stunning kitchen. The doors are usually kept closed to protect its contents from dust.

ABOVE RIGHT: I thought the little glass cabinet in this Dutch home was so sweet, especially with that little white deer peeking out from the top shelf. Vintage cabinets like this one are hard to find and you rarely stumble across them, but they can be reproduced if you know the style you want and you take your specs to a carpenter.

DECORATING KIDS' ROOMS

A child's bedroom can be such a rewarding room to decorate because you can express your love for them, think about your own childhood and what you'd like to pass on, add handmade touches that both you and your little one create together and let your colour and pattern desires run wild – kids love a fun room to play in and enjoy. Make it a point to really connect with your son or daughter, ask what he or she imagines in the room. Discuss what some of their favourite things are – animals, planes, dinosaurs, butterflies – and find ways to incorporate them in the scheme. Don't be tempted to pick on one thing and swamp the room with that theme though, however much enthusiasm they show – give them scope for their tastes to change and evolve over time. You can even get them involved by working on a moodboard together using photos that you ask them to pick from magazines so they can visually share their ideas. They are only young once, so have fun and enjoy the process!

ABOVE: This sweet space belongs to a little boy in London and he is quite a clever and creative little explorer according to his mother, Emma Cassi. I love how boxes on the wall are filled with favourite things and that pendants and lights are draped corner to corner, lending a carnival-like atmosphere. When styling your child's room, why not let them be your helper and ask for their creative input?

OPPOSITE: This nursery is simply the sweetest, isn't it? I met the little girl who sleeps here and she was as cute as you could imagine! When styling a nursery, incorporate what you believe will grow with your child, such as throws and quilts, artwork, cushions, curtains, flooring and storage pieces. Also remember that themed rooms are limiting and can be a bit overwhelming, so allow your child to grow into their own style and display things that they like later on, instead.

' Children love art projects and decorating can be an exciting one for them to explore, so get them involved early on! '

193

Your home is like your wardrobe

Decorating isn't done in a single day or even year; just as your wardrobe evolves, so will your interior surroundings. Once you have your basics in place you can build on them layer by layer, and after time has passed you may need to even replace those foundation pieces.

- Your wardrobe should include jeans that make your butt look good (always important!), a great blazer, a great coat, one good dress, a skirt, a pair of smart trousers and a few blouses that you mix and match as needed. You may have a party dress that you wear when you're invited out last minute or a killer pair of heels that dress up just about anything you put on. Decorating is much like your wardrobe, you first have to know and understand your body type, which cut and style of clothing looks best, your personal style, the colours that suit you. Then you can work in those foundation pieces (trousers, blouse, blazer, etc.) and build from there, layering in both essentials (shoes) and non-essentials (a ton of gorgeous bangles). Your focal point is usually your face, but you may also choose to highlight something you love about your body – your tiny waist or curvy hips, your broad shoulders (if you're a man!), your buff arms, etc.

- The same goes for your home. You should consider the architecture and what would look best in the space to complement that. The goal is to highlight what you love about the space whether it's the ceiling height, architectural details, great flooring or the gorgeous natural daylight, and conceal the rest, including the view of the neighbour's brick wall from your kitchen window and the popcorn-textured ceiling. Then you need to know your personal style and the colours that make you happiest, which also work in that particular room. From there, you list what foundation pieces you need in the space – a sofa, a bed frame, a wardrobe.

At that point, you layer in both the essentials (lighting) and non-essentials (that favourite piece of china to display on a shelf).

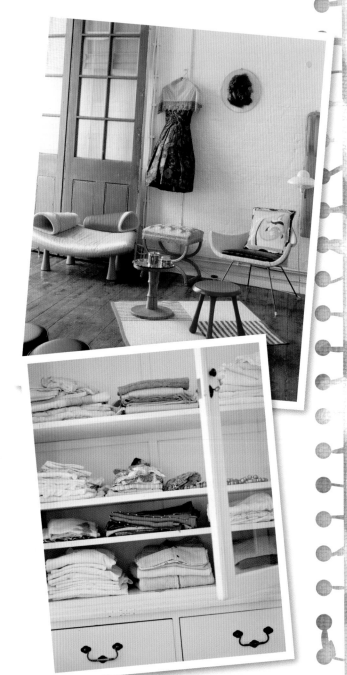

How will you dress your home?

It's interesting to view your home as you do your wardrobe, isn't it? As a process it's a lot more familiar to us as we all buy clothes. I find this approach makes it seem a lot more relaxing and fun – it is a much-needed break from all-or-nothing 'absolute' thinking. Those final decorating touches pull a room together. What do you want your room to say about you? How can you bring more of your story into your space? What are some tips that you've learned thus far that you'd like to use to personalize your home? List your ideas here.

Styling bookcases and shelves

Books bring a lot of heart into a home so it's important how we display and store them. A bookcase can quickly become visual noise, the room's ugly duckling, without any thought to style or cohesion in its arrangement. Chaotic shelves are stressful to look upon and can make even the most gorgeous room feel completely out of whack. Never fear! Taming the beast to transform it into a gorgeously curated display can be accomplished in a single afternoon and will make a noticeable difference. Here are some fun ways to create cohesion, add visual interest and have a little fun in the process. Have you ever thought to . . .

- Create a rainbow of books by arranging them by spine colour. Beginning from left to right, start with red and create a rainbow of books. While this does make title-browsing complicated since there is nothing tying the books together except colour, it does look great! I only organize my decorating books by colour on just two shelves for a little colour pop on my bookcase, but you can certainly colour code all of your books if you feel daring!

- Cover books with paper as you did in school; I like brown parcel paper. If your handwriting is good, use a metallic pen and write the book title in fancy writing on the spine. This project is great for smaller collections of books with worn-out covers that are all the same height, like paperbacks, for instance.

- Remove worn dust jackets to reveal, in most cases, a more attractive cover and spine that is worthy of display.

- Mix vertical rows with horizontal stacks, placing the best-looking book cover on top of the pile.

- Keep a shelf or two completely free of books to arrange a collection of pottery or another collection of things that you want to share.

- Reserve the top shelf for a collection – your prized collection of vintage fans, for instance. Keep some visual space between them so that your bookcase doesn't appear to have too much disproportionate volume on top.

- Alternate the height of your horizontal stacks, topping a few of them with a pretty object that relates to the arrangement somehow (colour, subject, texture, pattern, etc.).

- Mix in artwork, urns, a flower arrangement, sculptures, bowls, storage bins, magazine files, your stereo system and speakers, etc. A bookcase doesn't only have to hold books – in fact, it's more interesting if it doesn't!

- Group objects together in uneven numbers or in a single pair. Leave some breathing space between your groupings so objects stand out and don't feel crammed together.

- Keep books that you refer to and really love and sell, store, or donate the rest. You'll turn to them more frequently if the sheer quantity doesn't overwhelm you.

OPPOSITE: Grouping multiple objects on a bookcase is helpful for organization and more appealing visually than scattering items randomly. Collections kept together appear more streamlined. Grouping is the way to go when you have many things on display.

ART

LEFT: This graphic geometric art in the Brooklyn home of Nadia Yaron and Myriah Scruggs is stunning – it doesn't need to be surrounded by other pieces because it makes a strong presentation on its own. Artwork can bring energy, colour and a certain vibe to a space so it's wise to ensure that you pick what you are in love with.

OPPOSITE: Jean-Christophe Aumas transformed his photographs into works of art. He likes to lean his displays around his apartment, on tables and on the floor against walls, so that he can change his displays on a whim, and this is a flexible approach to display art.

Choosing art and displaying it is an exciting adventure – you can tell your personal story while also sharing the perspective of an artist whom you admire. Don't forget there also needs to be some relationship between your interior and the art in order to create harmony. Connecting the dots is best done through colour, but can also be accomplished through pattern. In the living room opposite a photograph with splashes of yellow highlights the same colour on a ceramic piece on a nearby table.

Hanging art salon style

It takes time, patience and practise to pull together your art in a pleasing way that enhances your home, but it's well worth the effort because it can be the difference between loving your space and feeling somewhat irritated and distanced from it. Let's make this process helpful and fun by reviewing the following shortcuts for grouping art with personality and style. Ready to face that blank wall with confidence? Good! Let's get started.

- When pulling together salon style, think of the story that you are trying to tell through the work so there is a sense of cohesion. Perhaps you are working from a specific colour palette, or you are going for a very graphic look, or maybe a specific theme along the lines of shapes (geometrics, for instance), people (nude studies, for instance), objects or nature.

- A good rule to follow when composing salon style is to either keep your work tight, which means the frames nearly touch, keep art and objects 4cm apart if you want a closer grouping or up to 8cm apart if you want the wall colour or pattern to show through between the frames. This breathing space is helpful, but take care to keep each piece an equal distance from the others so some aren't creating an unhealthy tension by being closer than others (appearing a bit wonky) or worse, spaced too far out from the others, which can make the arrangement look disconnected.

- Lay everything you love on the floor, framed, salon style, and see what works together – what makes sense visually – and don't be afraid to pull out pieces that don't fit the grouping. Take a photo so that you can refer to it once you begin grouping them on the wall. You can use blue painter's tape (doesn't leave marks) to position the work by creating an outline of each frame, or you can create silhouettes using brown paper to see how they work before using a hammer and nails.

- If you have tons of family photos but no clue how to make them work since they come in all sizes, colours and tones, try scanning them on your computer and converting them all into sepia, for instance, then framing them in the same colour frame, like black, to further marry them. (The shape is not important unless you want the arrangement to be very neat and clean.) You'd be surprised at how big a difference this will make and what a gorgeous wall you can create from images that were once mismatched and stuck in a drawer.

- It is common for people to hang their art too high. The centre of a painting or grouping should be at eye level. For instance, if you are hanging art on a wall where there is no furniture, hang the lowest piece around 1.5m from the floor. If you have a piece of furniture against the wall, like a sofa or headboard, it's a good idea to have the lowest piece of art around 20cm from the top of the furniture.

- If your art is better than your frames and your budget doesn't allow for you to invest in new ones, play them down by painting them all in the same colour (such as matt silver, grey, white, black lacquer, etc.) so that the art becomes the focal point. Even basic frames can look surprisingly chic once you've unified the colour. White frames with white mounts really help art to stand out, silver frames can dress up your wall with a little sparkle and black can be very graphic and bold.

Can I hang anything on the wall and call it art?

A wall is a blank canvas, your canvas, and you are free to create your own artistic arrangement of things – expensive things, cheap things, hand-me-downs, found items – whatever works for you, so go for it. If you believe something to be beautiful, personal, appealing or of more than ordinary significance then you can rightfully term that item as art in my opinion.

- Art should reflect your personality and be something that you connect to, something meaningful, perhaps with a sense of history or even a piece that encourages you to dream bigger for the future. Art should be deeply personal and definitely something that makes you feel positive whenever you look at it. It can be a framed bib that your grandmother made for you as a baby, your children's artwork framed, pieces of lace from your mother's wedding gown or a vintage oil painting that you scored at a local flea market. The bottom line is that if you like it then you should find a place to display it in your home.

- If you don't own many paintings, drawings, prints, photography or framed work in general, maybe those things aren't for you and you need to try a different approach. Opt for branches that you can paint and perhaps hang things from (like feathers or butterflies or even handmade leaves that you can make using fabric), fallen antlers, hooks with your favourite scarves artfully draped or showing your most gorgeous coats and dresses. Empty frames can be made into pinboards with your brooches and necklaces tacked inside, or try a collection of mirrors. Art doesn't have to be in a frame or signed by an artist!

- Collect over time – avoid buying all of your art in a single day. Instead, collect a nice grouping of things gradually and then you can pull together a salon-style wall or expand what you currently have by adding in additional pieces.

- Empty frames are always fun to hang! Inside, on the wall, you can use Japanese masking tape to attach a favourite image or several. It's fun to experiment with different looks and you can change the art inside of your frames very easily without removing the frames – just remove and tape in different images as you collect and are inspired by new finds.

- Art doesn't always need to be on a wall or even framed. You can lean it against the wall along the top of your sideboard, prop it against a wall on the floor, arrange it on a table 'altar' style, on a windowsill, on a mantel, inside a fireplace (preferably an unused one). Bring in other items, too, such as stacked books, a disco ball, tons of candles in decorative holders. A collection of glass domes on a tabletop could make beautiful cases for a collection of coral or taxidermy, for instance, if that's your thing.

- Often a beautiful window showcasing a gorgeous view is art in its own right. You can use hooks to fix transparent wire to the frame, and hang crystals, ornaments or flower vases to give a window a more creative touch. You can also use a string to create a horizontal display of inspirational things clipped onto it – postcards, photographs, ribbons, etc. Bunting looks lovely draped across a window, too, especially in a children's room or in a dining room during a party. If you have windowsills, consider using those as a place to show favourite things, from ceramics to wooden sculptures, or vintage bottles with fresh flowers.

In closing . . .

Dear Readers,

Thank you for spending time flipping through these pages, reading here and there, jotting down your own notes and then going off to daydream, plan and create. Knowing that you have my book in your hands deeply touches my heart. This book is my personal approach to decorating but you may have already carved out your own approach by mixing the steps up or by taking some and leaving others. We all have to find the recipe for decorating within ourselves. I can guide you but I'll never tell you – your heart will do that as you open your mind to gain ideas and inspiration. It will lead the way, trust me.

I've left you with a small gift – the French Fold book jacket. You can turn it inside out, iron it (use a cotton cloth between the iron and paper and keep the iron on a very low setting), and frame it for your home or pin it in your office for inspiration. I've not yet come across a French Fold in a decorating book that could double as art, so I hope that you'll enjoy this small gift for your lovely nest.

When it comes to decorating please remember to not be hard on yourself and to take an organic approach that stems from the heart. I hope that this book has given you a good feeling about your home and the ability that you have to pull together rooms that you cherish. Don't miss out on the opportunity that you have to make a personal connection to yourself and then your space – decorating can do that for you. It's a form of creativity that can allow you to soar to new heights. A home should be uniquely you. It should contain those you love, memories that you cherish, items that connect you to your past, objects that can inspire today and possessions that will carry you into the future. Your home is your canvas – create something wonderful!

Happy Decorating!

Love
Holly

PS If you create moodboards using some of the ideas in this book, will you share them with me? You can tweet, Facebook or use Pinterest or Instagram. I'll find your images if you use hashtag #DecorateWorkshop. You are also welcome to join or post them to my Facebook page www.facebook.com/DecorateBook. Thank you!

Directory

Some of my favourite stores and suppliers

ABC CARPET & HOME
abchome.com

ANTHROPOLOGIE
anthropologie.com

ASTIER DE VILLATTE
astierdevillate.com

ATELIER ABIGAIL AHERN
atelierabigailahern.com

BALLARD DESIGNS
ballarddesigns.com

BHLDN
bhldn.com

BODIE AND FOU
bodieandfou.com

CATH KIDSTON
cathkidston.co.uk

CB2
cb2.com

CRATE & BARREL
crateandbarrel.com

DESIGNERS GUILD
designersguild.com

DESIGN WITHIN REACH
dwr.com

FARROW & BALL
farrow-ball.com

FERM LIVING
ferm-living.com

FISHS EDDY
fishseddy.com

HEATH CERAMICS
heathceramics.com

HOUSE DOCTOR
housedoctor.dk

KERRY CASSILL
kerrycassill.com

JOHN DERIAN
johnderian.com

JOHN LEWIS
johnlewis.co.uk

JONATHAN ADLER
jonathanadler.com

KNACK STUDIOS
knackstudios.com

LIBERTY
liberty.co.uk

MERCI
merci-merci.com

MUROBOND PAINT
murobond.com.au

NORMANN COPENHAGEN
normann-copenhagen.com

OCHRE
ochre.net

ORLA KIELY
orlakiely.com

PETERSHAM NURSERIES
petershamnurseries.co.uk

POLS POTTEN
polspotten.nl

RE
re-foundobjects.com

RICE
rice.dk

ROYAL COPENHAGEN
royalcopenhagen.com

SELFRIDGES
selfridges.co.uk

SHABBY CHIC COUTURE
rachelashwellshabbychiccouture.com

ST JUDES
stjudes.co.uk

TERRAIN AT STYER'S
shopterrain.com

THE CONRAN SHOP
conran.com

THE SOCIETY, INC.
thesocietyinc.com.au

VV ROULEAUX
vvrouleaux.com

WEST ELM
westelm.com

Some of my favourite lifestyle magazines
from around the world

VTWONEN, THE NETHERLANDS vtwonen.nl
101 WOONIDEEEN, THE NETHERLANDS 101woonideeen.nl
SELVEDGE, UK selvedge.org
ELLE DECORATION, UK elledecoration.co.uk
LIVINGETC, UK housetohome.co.uk/livingetc
MOLLIE MAKES, UK molliemakes.themakingspot.com
LIVING AT HOME, GERMANY livingathome.de
ESSEN UND TRINKEN, GERMANY essen-und-trinken.de
SCHOENER WOHNEN, GERMANY schoener-wohnen.de
LIVING AND MORE, GERMANY livingandmore.de
LUNA, GERMANY lunamag.de
WE LOVE LIVING, GERMANY weloveliving.de
DONNA HAY, AUSTRALIA donnahay.com.au/magazine
REAL LIVING, AUSTRALIA homes.ninemsn.com.au/real-living
INSIDE OUT, AUSTRALIA homelife.com.au/magazine/
inside+out
COUNTRY STYLE, AUSTRALIA homelife.com.au/magazine/
country+style
FRANKIE, AUSTRALIA frankie.com.au
JAMIE, UNITED STATES jamieoliver.com/magazine
COUNTRY LIVING, UNITED STATES countryliving.com
ANTHOLOGY, UNITED STATES anthologymag.com
MARTHA STEWART LIVING, UNITED STATES
marthastewart.com
MARTHA STEWART WEDDINGS, UNITED STATES
marthastewartweddings.com
ELLE DECOR, UNITED STATES elledecor.com
BETTER HOMES & GARDENS, UNITED STATES bhg.com
REAL SIMPLE, UNITED STATES realsimple.com
DOMINO dominomag.com
MILK, FRANCE milkmagazine.net
BOLIGLIV, DENMARK boligliv.dk
RUM, DENMARK rumid.dk
UPPERCASE, CANADA uppercasegallery.ca
HOUSE & HOME, CANADA houseandhome.com

Some of my favourite e-magazines

LONNY lonnymag.com
MATCHBOOK matchbookmag.com
RUE ruemag.com
SWEET PAUL sweetpaulmag-digital.com
HEART HOME hearthomemag.co.uk
EST estemag.com
GATHERINGS heatherspriggs.com/gatherings-magazine
91 91magazine.co.uk
WHAT LIBERTY ATE whatlibertyate.com/magazine
STYLED asubtlerevelry.com/styled
PAPER RUNWAY paperrunway.com
PAPIER MACHE papier-mache.com.au/magazine
IVY & PIPER ivyandpiper.com.au
ADORE adoremagazine.com
CELLARDOOR cellardoormagazine.co.uk
SMALL MAGAZINE smallmagazine.net
LA PETITE MAGAZINE lapetitemag.com
UTTERLY ENGAGED utterlyengaged.com
MAEVE MAGAZINE maevemagazine.com
LMNOP lmnop.com.au/buy
SISTER MAGAZINE sister-mag.com
TOFFEE toffeemag.com
N.E.E.T. neetmagazine.com
BABIEKINS babiekinsmag.com
TINY & LITTLE tinyandlittle.com.au/magazine
REVERIE reveriemag.com
WAYFARE wayfaremag.com

Some great places to buy art

etsy.com
dawanda.de
eBay.com
flea markets
junk shops
craigslist.org
beholder-art.com
student art fairs at local art schools
artomat.org
folksy.com
ugallery.com
bigcartel.com

Photo credits

Every effort has been made to trace the copyright holders, architects and designers. We apologise in advance for any unintentional omission and would be pleased to insert acknowledgement in any subsequent edition.

Artworks are by Sanantha Hahn
All photographs were taken by Debi Treloar, unless otherwise stated.

Page 1 Thorsten Becker; p 2 Emma Cassi, London; p 3 Desiree Groenendal, Amsterdam; p 4 - 7 - 8 Thorsten Becker; p 13 top row left & centre Desiree Groenendal, Amsterdam; p 13 top row right & centre row left Randi Brookman Harris New York; p 13 centre row centre Emma Cassi, London; p 13 centre row right & bottom row left Desiree Groenendal, Amsterdam; p 13 bottom row centre Emma Cassi, London; p 13 bottom row right Laure du Chatenet, Paris; p 14 left Astier de Villatte, Paris; p 14 centre Randi Brookman Harris, New York; p 14 right Sania Pell, London; p 15 left Iris Rietbergen, Amsterdam; p 15 centre & right Thorsten Becker; p 17 Jean-Christophe Aumas, Paris; p 21, 22, 29, 35, 41, 61, 64, 65, 71, 75, 79, 83, 204, 205, 206, 207, 208 Liberty; p 23 top Leslie Shewring, Rancho Palos Verdes, CA; p 27 top left & right Astier de Villatte, Paris; p 27 bottom left Simon Upton / The Interior Archive; p 27 Emma Cassi, London; p 29 inset bottom right Thorsten Becker; p 30 James Leland Day, Paris; p 31 Jean-Christophe Aumas, Paris; p 33 top row left Stephanie Rammeloo, Amsterdam; p 33 top row centre Anita Kaushal, London; p 33 top row right Emma Lee, East Sussex; p 33 centre row left Laure du Chatenet, Paris; p 33 centre row centre James Leland Day, Paris; p 33 centre row right Claus and Heidi Robenhagen, Copenhagen; p 33 bottom row left Laure du Chatenet, Paris; p 33 bottom row centre Jean-Christophe Aumas, Paris; p 33 bottom row right Claus and Heidi Robenhagen, Copenhagen; p 36 Emma Lee, East Sussex; p 37 left James Leland Day, Paris; p 37 right Emma Lee, East Sussex; p 38 moodboard by Holly Becker; p 39 Emma Cassi, London; p 42 Desiree Groenendal, Amsterdam; p 43 Emma Cassi, London; p 44 moodboard by Holly Becker; p 45 Emma Lee, East Sussex; p 46 - 47 Tinta Luhrmann, Amsterdam; p 47 Desiree Groenendal, Amsterdam; p 48 left Emma Lee, East Sussex; p 48 right Allyn Naomi Yamanouchi, New York; p 49 Lesley Townsend, New York; p 52 - 53 Jean-Christophe Aumas, Paris; p 54 – 55 James Leland Day, Paris; p 56 left Brandi Becker, New York; p 56 – 57 Allyn Naomi Yamanouchi, New York; p 57 right Emma Lee, East Sussex; p 58 left James Leland Day, Paris; p 58 right Brandi Becker, New York; p 59 Allyn Naomi Yamanouchi, New York; p 61 inset bottom right Brandi Becker, New York; p 63 top row left William Waldron / The Interior Archive; p 63 top row centre Desiree Groenendal, Amsterdam; p 63 top row right Laure du Chatenet, Paris; p 63 centre row left Tinta Luhrmann, Amsterdam; p 63 centre row centre Lesley Townsend, New York; p 63 centre row right Allyn Naomi Yamanouchi, New York; p 63 bottom row left Marc and Melissa Palazzo, Orange County, CA; p 63 bottom row centre Lesley Townsend, New York; p 63 bottom row right Iris Rietbergen, Amsterdam; p 66 Emma Lee, East Sussex; p 67 top Tinta Luhrmann, Amsterdam; p 67 bottom Emma Lee, East Sussex; p 72 left Emma Lee, East Sussex; p 72 right Tinta Luhrmann, Amsterdam, p 73 William Waldron / The Interior Archive; p 74 Tinta Lurhmann, Amsterdam; p 75 background Liberty; p 77 top row left & centre Randi Brookman Harris, New York; p 77 top row right Emma Lee, East Sussex; p 77 centre row left Randi Brookman Harris, New York; p 77 centre row centre Lesley Townsend, New York; p 77 centre row right: photographer: Thorsten Becker home of: Tinna Pedersen, Hannover, Germany p 77 bottom row left Emma Lee, East Sussex; p 77 bottom row centre Emma Cassi, London; p 77 bottom row right Lesley Townsend, New York; p 78 Simon Upton / The Interior Archive; p 81 Iris Rietbergen, Amsterdam; p 85 top Laure du Chatenet, Paris; p 85 centre Simon Upton / The Interior Archive; p 85 bottom Emma Lee, East Sussex; p 86 left Brandi Becker, New York; p 86 right Emma Lee, East Sussex; p 87 left James Leland Day, Paris; p 89 top row left Lesley Townsend , New York; p 89 top row centre Desiree Groenendal, Amsterdam; p 89 centre row left Simon Upton / The Interior Archive; p 89 centre row centre Mads Hagedorn-Olsen and Karen Kjaelgard-Larsen, Copenhagen; p 89 centre row right Desiree Groenendal, Amsterdam; p 89 bottom row left Simon Upton / The Interior Archive; p 89 bottom row centre Randi Brookman Harris, New York; p 89 bottom row right Jean-Christophe Aumas, Paris; p 90, 91,119, 142, 151, 158, 165, 174, 181, 194, 195, 196, 201, Quadrille Fabrics; p 93 inset top Jean Christophe Aumas, Paris; p 93 inset bottom William Waldron / The Interior Archive; page 95 lower righ: Thorsten Becker; p 96 – 97 – 98 – 99 Emma Lee, East Sussex; p 100 – 101 – 102 – 103 Laure du Chatenet, Paris; p 104 – 105 Iris Rietbergen, Amsterdam; p 106 – 107 Nadia Yaron & Myriah Scruggs, New York; p 108 – 109 Iris Rietbergen, Amsterdam; p 110 – 111 Desiree Groenendal, Amsterdam; p 112 – 113 – 114 -115 Emma Lee, East Sussex; p 116 – 117 Laure du Chatenet, Paris; p 121 top row left & top row centre Mads Hagedorn-Olsen & Karen Kjaeldgard-Larsen, Copenhagen; p 121 top row right Brandi Becker, New York; p 121 centre row left Marc & Melissa Palazzo, Orange County; p 121 centre row centre Emma Lee, East Sussex; p 121 centre row right Jean Christophe Aumas, Paris; p 121 bottom row left Marc and Melissa Palazzo, Orange County p 121 bottow row centre Lesley Townsend, New York; p 121 bottom row right Nadia Yaron & Myriah Scruggs, New York; p123 left & right moodboards by Holly Becker and photographed by Thorsten Becker; p125 moodboard by Holly Becker; p 126 moodboard by Holly Becker, photographed by Thorsten Becker; p129 moodboard by Holly Becker, photographed by Thorsten Beckerp 130/131 moodboard by Holly Becker, photographed by Thorsten Becker; p133 top row left & centre Sania Pell, London; p 133 top row right Astier de Villatte, Paris; p 133 centre row left Lesley Townsend, New York; p 133 centre row centre Emma Cassi, London; p 133 centre row right Tinta Luhrmann, Amsterdam; p 133 bottom row left Sania Pell, London; p 133 bottom row centre Desiree Groenendal, Amsterdam; p 133 bottom row right Sania Pell; p 135 left & right William Waldron / The Interior Archive; p136 moodboard by Holly Becker, photographed by Thorsten Becker; p 138 Randi Brookman Harris, New York; p 139 William Waldron / The Interior Archive; p 140 – 141 Jean-Christophe Aumas, Paris; p 143 top left Frederic Vasseur / Cote Paris; p 143 top right Fritz Von Den Schulenberg / The Interior Archive; p 143 bottom left Simon Upton / The Interior Archive; p 143 bottom right Nadia Yaron & Myriah Scruggs, New York; p 144 left Emma Cassi, London; p 144 right Jean-Christophe Aumas, Paris; p 145 Jean- Christophe Aumas, Paris; p 148 left Brandi Becker, New York; p 148 right Emma Cassi, London; p 149 left Allyn Naomi Yamanouchi, New York; p 149 right Nadia Yaron & Myriah Scruggs, New York; p 150 Randi Brookman Harris, New York; p 152 – 153 Roger Davies / The Interior Archive; p 154 Nadia Yaron & Myriah Scruggs, New York; p 154 – 155 William Waldron / The Interior Archive; p 155 Sania Pell, London; p 156 – 157 Iris Rietbergen, Amsterdam; p 159 Tinta Luhrmann, Amsterdam; p 161: left and right: Yvonne Eijkenduijn, Lommel, Belgium; p 163 Desiree Groenendal, Amsterdam; p 167 top row left & centre Brandi Becker, New York; p 167 top row right Randi Brookman Harris, New York; p 167 centre row left Sania Pell, London; p 167 centre row centre Iris Rietbergen, Amsterdam; p 167 centre row right Randi Brookman Harris, New York; p 167 bottom row left & centre Iris Rietbergen, Amsterdam;   p 167 bottom row right Tinta Luhrmann, Amsterdam; p 168 Brandi Becker, New York; p 169 Nadia Yaron & Myriah Scruggs, New York; p 170 James Leland Day, Paris; p 171 - 172 moodboard by Holly Becker; p 173 James Leland Day, Paris; p 175 Emma Lee, East Sussex; p 176 – 177 Emma Cassi, London; p 178 -179 Tinta Luhrmann, Amsterdam; p 183 – 184 Emma Cassi, London; p 185 Emma Lee, East Sussex; p 186 left & right Emma Cassi; p 187 left Sania Pell, London; p 187 right Emma Cassi, London; p 188 Jean-Christophe Aumas, Paris; p 189 Lesley Townsend, New York; p 190 Jean-Christophe Aumas, Paris; p 191 Tinta Luhrmann, Amsterdam; p 192 - 193 Emma Cassi, London; p 194 inset top Simon Upton / The Interior Archive; p 194 inset bottom Anita Kaushal, London; p 197 Randi Brookman Harris, New York; p 198 Nadia Yaron & Myriah Scruggs, New York; p 199 Jean-Christophe Aumas, Paris; p 200 top left Simon Upton / The Interior Archive; p 200 bottom left James Leland Day, Paris; p 200 bottom right Laure du Chatenet, Paris; p 203 Brandi Brookman Harris, New York; p 208 inset bottom Thorsten Becker.

JACKET CREDITS

Front cover images: Moodboard by Holly Becker, photographed by Thorsten Becker; bottom left Emma Lee, East Sussex; bottom right inset Marc & Melissa Palazzo, Orange County; bottom right top Charlotte Hedeman Gueniau, Kertminde, Denmark.

Reverse cover images: Top row image 1 moodboard designed by Holly Becker; image 2 Allyn Naomi Yamanouchi, New York; image 3 Astier de Villatte, Paris; image 4 Nadia Yaron & Myriah Scruggs, New York; image 5 Jean-Christophe Aumas, Paris. Centre row image 2 Emma Lee, East Sussex; image 3 Randi Brookman Harris, New York; image 4 Mads Hagedorn-Olsen & Karen Kjaeldgard-Larsen, Copenhagen, image 5 David Butler/ David & Amy Butler, Granville, Ohio; moodboard designed by Holly Becker.
Bottom row: image 1; moodboard designed by Holly Becker; image 2 Jean-Christophe Aumas, Paris; image 3 Tinta Luhrmann, Amsterdam; image 3 Laure Du Chatenet, Paris.

Back cover and spine: fabric by Amy Butler Design
Back cover images: Top right James Leland Day, Paris; bottom left Emma Lee, East Sussex; bottom right Desiree Groenendal, Amsterdam.
French folds fabric 'Hedgerow" by Angie Lewin for St Jude's www.stjudes.co.uk